THE HISTORICAL ELEMENT IN RELIGION

Clement C. J. Webb

THE HISTORICAL ELEMENT
IN RELIGION

LEWIS FRY LECTURES

Delivered at the
UNIVERSITY OF BRISTOL
1934

by

CLEMENT C. J. WEBB, F.B.A.

*Honorary Fellow of Oriel College, Oxford, and
sometime Oriel Professor of the Philosophy
of the Christian Religion*

LONDON
GEORGE ALLEN & UNWIN LTD
MUSEUM STREET

FIRST PUBLISHED IN 1935

PRINTED IN GREAT BRITAIN BY
UNWIN BROTHERS LTD., WOKING

PREFACE

THE writing of this book was due to the invitation by which I was honoured a year ago to deliver lectures before the University of Bristol on the Lewis Fry foundation. The first four chapters of it contain the substance of the lectures delivered in response to this invitation; while the fifth was added as an attempt to answer the question, put to me after their delivery, how I should apply the principles enunciated therein to such alleged historical facts as have been generally believed among Christians as belonging to the substance of their religious creed, or at least as presupposed by the organization of their religious life. I will only add that I hope my readers will not assume that the correctness of my views as to the nature of the Historical Element in Religion stand or fall with my own or any other particular opinions concerning the historicity of the narrative to which the final chapter refers.

C. C. J. W.

MARSTON, OXFORD
  February 1935

CONTENTS

THE HISTORICAL ELEMENT IN RELIGION

I

In the first of four Lectures in which I propose to say what I have to say about the Historical Element in Religion I shall attempt to fix the meaning of the expression; in the second to examine the position actually assigned to the historical element in religion generally, and especially in that religion with which I myself and probably the majority of my readers are best acquainted, namely, the Christian; in the third to discuss the arguments of some among those who, whether from a strictly religious or from a philosophical point of view, have depreciated the importance of the historical element relatively to other factors in the life of religion; and in the fourth and last to submit for your consideration certain conclusions which I have myself been led to adopt as to the place rightly to be assigned to this element therein.

I shall then begin by asking you to put to yourselves the question what meaning is to be attached to this phrase, "The Historical Element in Religion." The

expression may recall to some the title of a well-known
book by the late Baron Friedrich von Hügel, *The
Mystical Element in Religion*; and those who happen
to have read that book will remember that the author
distinguishes three elements in all religion, of which
that which he calls the Mystical is one, the others
being designated by him as the Intellectual and the
Institutional respectively. It is not my present purpose
either to defend or to criticize this particular classification of the factors which go to constitute the kind of
experience to which the name of Religion is given.
Von Hügel himself sometimes uses the word Historical
as equivalent to Institutional. I shall not, however,
be careful to keep to this usage, but shall make an
independent attempt to ascertain the meaning which
may be most conveniently given to the word in this
connexion. It may, however, be useful to remark that
neither in studying a predominantly mystical nor in
studying a predominantly intellectual type of religion
can we dispense altogether with a reference to the
past history of the religious community in which they
appear. At first sight one might perhaps expect this
to be of little importance in the former case, for the
mystic's experience is taken (by the mystic himself
at any rate) to be an immediate contact with a present
reality, and he is thus apt to be comparatively in-

different to evidence respecting the experience of others in the past. Yet there is much in the language employed by mystical writers which is unintelligible apart from some acquaintance with the history of the religion which they profess or in which they have been bred; and this is because that history always exercises a considerable influence over the form taken by their own experience. Again, a man whose religion is mainly speculative or philosophical, a religion in which the "Intellectual Element" predominates, may indeed be relatively unconcerned with the historical truth of the traditions associated with the language in which he is accustomed to express it, and may even insist that religion is not at all interested in maintaining it. Yet we must not forget that, at certain times and in certain places, the chief use made of the intellect in the service of religion has been in the study of these associated traditions and in the defence of their credibility; nor is the independence of them assumed by the philosophical exponent of the religion with which they are associated always as complete as he may, quite sincerely, suppose it to be.

What I am now asking you to do is to consider with me the manner and degree in which our religious experience, whatever its special character may be, is affected by our knowledge or belief in regard to facts of the kind that fall within the purview of the historian.

Among such facts are no doubt those which constitute the past history, whether of any particular religion or of religion in general. But when we speak of the Historical Element in Religion, or in some particular religion, we are not, I think, thinking primarily of these as such. Of every mode of human behaviour it would be possible to write a history, if only sufficient evidence about its antecedents were forthcoming; and religious behaviour is no exception to this rule. It has been, in my judgment, a mistake made by many "anthropological" students of religion to think that it can be explained, wholly or chiefly, by what we may call, in this sense, its "history"; so that, when one knows or suspects that the form of some religious custom or practice is determined by some past belief which the person now following that custom or practice does not hold, nothing is to be seen in it but a survival in present behaviour of the effects of some obsolete way of thinking or mode of life, and the treatment of it as possessing any further value may be safely dismissed as due to mere irrational habit.

No one would suppose that, if it could be shown that the violinist's bow had been evolved from the

primitive weapon so called, any light would be thereby
thrown upon the music which he plays; still less that
nothing more was to be found in that music than a
"survival" of savage warfare. No doubt the very fact
that the mistake, as I take it to be, is frequently made
in the one case and not in the other is itself to be
accounted for by what may be called the conservatism
of religion, which tends to attribute an importance
to the following of tradition less frequently attached
thereto in the domain of art; in other words, by the
circumstance that the "historical element" plays in
religion a larger part than it plays in art. But the
"historical element in religion" is not the past history
of religion as such, though the importance of the
historical element in religion is due in part to the fact
that a conscious interest in the past is characteristic
of the religious man's outlook as it is not in that of
the artist.

We are coming nearer to our proper subject when
we note this difference between the religious man and
the artist. All distinctively human behaviour has, I
think we may confidently affirm, a social aspect. But
among the various activities in which men engage
there are some from which this social aspect seems to
be inseparable, since they are explicitly directed
towards the life of the group or community of which

the agent is a member. It is not, indeed, necessary to follow the French sociologist Durkheim and his school in considering religion as a function of society in so strict a sense that we must regard as illusory the attribution to any object of religious worship of a reality independent of the emotion excited in the members of a group by the consciousness of sharing a common life with their fellow-members thereof. My reasons for dissenting from this view I have attempted to set forth in detail elsewhere.[1] But, without adopting the position of Durkheim, we may yet unhesitatingly assent to the statement that the intimate association of religion with what we may call the social conscious-ness of men is a fact which no student of human history can fail to observe. So far from Religion being essentially, in a frequently quoted phrase of Professor Whitehead's, "what the individual does with his own solitariness,"[2] it is obvious that by far the greater part of those activities which would be generally reckoned religious has been, as a matter of fact, carried on by men as members, and consciously members, of some community—a tribe or a nation, a church or a sect; and that, in the earlier stages of human development, such activities have most often been explicitly directed

[1] See *Group Theories of Religion and the Individual*, Allen & Unwin, 1916.   [2] *Religion in the Making*, p. 16.

towards securing what is conceived to be the interest of a community. It is, no doubt, true that, from a very early period, if not from the first, the initiative in religion seems to belong to exceptional individuals, set apart from their fellows by peculiarities which suggest that they have access to a world other than that of everyday life. It is true also that, as is pointed out in Dr. Heiler's classical book on Prayer,[1] the spontaneous cry of the solitary human being in trouble to "one above" seems to be due to a natural impulse independent of beliefs about the particular spirits or gods whose names may be connected with his tribal ceremonies. Yet, if asked to name the Being to whom his appeal was made, he would probably mention some traditional forefather of his race; and it would be with some such name, familiar to his fellow-tribesmen, that the primitive prophet, mystic, medicine-man, or whatever we are to call him, supposes himself or is supposed by others to have to do in the trances or ecstasies, real or pretended, which cause him to be regarded as an organ of revelation from some higher sphere of being.

Now an historical element in religion, in the sense in which we shall in this course of lectures be engaged in discussing its nature and importance, is an element

[1] See especially *Das Gebet*, pp. 122, 123.

in religion precisely in consequence of the social character which belongs to religion as a mode of behaviour or activity carried on by men as members of a community. The explanation of religious actions —in answer to the enquiry, "What mean you by this service?"[1]—must be given to young or newly joined members of the community in terms which imply that the community had a past in which those who then belonged to it did or suffered or ordained something to justify the action that is here and now performed or required. It belongs to the experience of becoming a member of a community, or of realizing that one has been born into a community, that one identifies oneself with it, and thinks of a past which one does not oneself remember as yet in some sense one's own because it was the community's of which one is a member. One cannot doubt that it is just in the sense of belonging to a community—tribe or family or voluntary brotherhood—which has a past not remembered by oneself, yet of which one is told by those who themselves remember it or have been in like manner told of it by others, that there first arises in the human mind that interest in the past which is the presupposition of all history. Moreover, in all likelihood, this interest is first aroused in connexion

[1] Exod. xii. 26.

with acts which may be properly called religious. For they are expressions of emotions excited by the consciousness of one's own union with a larger life, through which one comes into touch with those encompassing powers and influences upon accommodation to which one's welfare ultimately depends, and thus have the character of combined *ultimacy* and *intimacy* which, as I have elsewhere contended,[1] is the hall-mark of religion. We may, I think, say with some assurance that that interest in the past which is the presupposition of all history is not merely from the first associated with religion, but has its very springs in an experience which is essentially religious. In other words, not only is there always an historical element in religion, but it is, in all probability, as an element in religion that history makes its first appearance in human thought.

Religion, normally, at any rate, is communal; and, because communal, traditional; and, because traditional, historical; and, while it remains communal, it must remain traditional and therefore historical. But, as we watch the evolution of religion, whether in the history of the world or in the life of an individual soul, we shall find manifesting themselves within

[1] See *Religion and Theism* (Allen & Unwin), p. 15. Cp. *In Spirit and in Truth* (Hodder & Stoughton), pp. 215 ff.

religion factors which may tend to the proportional diminution of the historical element, and eventually cause those differences of emphasis upon it, those divergences of opinion as to its importance, which have come to play so large a part in the theological discussions of the modern world.

Such a factor is an increased sense of individual personality, conscience, responsibility, and, in intimate connexion therewith, of an individual relation to God. For this, by throwing into the background the consciousness of dependence on the mediation of the community and intensifying the immediate perception of that which is "the heart and rule of life"[1] (whether envisaged as "transcendent" or as "immanent") tends to weaken interest in what is regarded as belonging to hearsay and to the past as distinguished from what is actual and present. This factor can, of course, be recognized a very long way back in the history of religion, and has played a part of the highest importance in that of the great historical religions which have challenged the allegiance of mankind and not only that of some particular people. Far more recent and rarer in its appearance is the disinterested interest (if I may be permitted the bull) in historical truth for its own sake, apart from any satisfaction to be afforded

[1] Swinburne, *Erechtheus*, 1748.

to religious or patriotic sentiment and from any practical application to be made of its lessons. When this interest has become prominent among followers of a religion, the effect of historical criticism, conducted in this spirit, upon the accounts of its own past preserved in the traditions of a community is apt to cast so much doubt upon them as to induce a desire, by rendering the religion as far as possible independent of these accounts, to secure it from the consequences of the loss of credit to which, when subjected to the strict examination of dispassionate scholars, they may probably be exposed.

The actual effects of such critical examination of records and traditions will of course vary in particular cases in correspondence with the trustworthiness of the traditions themselves and of the importance attached by the authorities of the religious communities to the acceptance of them. My second Lecture will be concerned with this latter consideration; while the investigation of the historical value of particular stories or documents is not my business in this present course. But the point which I desire to make in this first Lecture is that, in order to understand the place of the historical element in religion, we should do well to dismiss for the moment from our minds the thought of history as an objective record of past events, such

as is the ideal of many modern scholars: a record
unaffected by any interest in one rather than another
of the persons, parties, or communities whose conflicts
are described therein, and nowhere betraying the
political or confessional attachments of its authors, any
more than would the memoirs contributed by mathe-
maticians or physicists to the journals of scientific
societies. Whether this should indeed be the historian's
ideal I do not here enquire; but it is certainly not by
taking "history" in this sense that we shall put ourselves into a position to appreciate the importance of
the historical element in religion. We should rather
begin by thinking of the sentiment (a sentiment which
has in all probability often as a matter of fact originally
determined the career of the most dispassionate of
historical scholars) for a past as belonging to oneself
—or perhaps it would be more accurate to say, for
oneself as belonging to a past—which is found in those
to whom the life of a community to which they themselves belong—be it family or town, province or
country, school or college, club or regiment, party or
church, or whatever it may be—is a real life continually
apprehended by them as *their own*.

This kind of sentiment may be present in different
degrees of strength in different persons. There are
those in whom it seems almost or quite lacking; many

in whom it can be occasionally aroused, but over whom it exerts no important influence; others again in whom it attains to an even passionate intensity. But some measure of it is a normal attribute of humanity, after a certain stage of intellectual development has been reached.

Such a sentiment for a past felt as one's own, though not remembered by oneself as an individual, is certainly not an interest in the objective history which the modern scholar regards it as his ideal to discover. It makes, indeed, no pretence to be such. Yet (and this is the problem which makes an estimate of the place of the historical element in religion so important to the modern theologian) it cannot be wholly unaffected by investigations conducted by the devotees of that ideal. Doubt cast by these upon the accepted account of that past which one feels as bound up with oneself is highly disturbing. Whether one is prepared to repel it without examination as profane or unpatriotic, or is driven to explore the evidence in the hope of showing it to be unfounded, or is compelled by recognition of its justification to abandon, in theory or in practice or in both, allegiance to the community which seems to be at least suspected, if not convicted, of imposture in its claims—in any case such doubt does not leave untouched the lives of those who have become aware that it is entertained.

But it will be well to consider somewhat more closely in what way it actually touches their life. We will leave on one side for the moment cases in which it is held as an article of religious faith that a particular book, containing what purports to be historical information, is inspired and infallible, so that to doubt of the truth of the information to be found therein is to call in question an integral part of one's religious creed. We shall have to advert to such cases hereafter, but they only cover a part of the field with which we are now concerned. Apart from any such belief in the infallibility of a professedly historical narrative, it is, I think, plain that it must be a real shock to men whose aims and ideals are associated with a certain conception of the community whereof they are members—a conception probably involving a pride in the achievements of its earlier members and, in any case, including a belief that it has played a certain part in the world and stands in certain relations to other communities— to find this conception regarded as baseless. An individual who suddenly discovers that he is not the child of those whom he has always taken for granted were his parents may very likely experience an emotional *bouleversement* seriously affecting his whole future life. Will not those be in an analogous situation who, having been penetrated with the conviction that they are the heirs of certain traditions which have hitherto moulded their characters and determined their reaction to their environment, discover that these traditions rest upon no assured foundation?

It must have been difficult for a patriotic Swiss to accept without demur the judgment of historical scholars that William Tell never existed, and that his story is a local adaptation of an ancient legend current in many places other than Switzerland. But the Swiss are not called upon to doubt the general truth of the tradition that their fathers won their freedom from the tyranny of their feudal overlords by a brave resistance in which heroic leaders sacrificed themselves for the common cause. It may, no doubt, be said that, were the whole of what was believed to be the history of Switzerland proved to be based upon deliberate forgery, the existing freedom and civilization enjoyed to-day by the Swiss people would none the less be worthy of their devotion; just as the poetical merit of Virgil's *Aeneid* and Horace's *Odes* would be none the less real were they in fact, as the celebrated Père Hardouin held, the production of mediaeval monks masquerading as ancient pagans; or, to come nearer home, as that of Shakespeare's plays would remain unaffected though they were proved to have been written by Bacon. Even though it should be admitted that, without the belief in the supposedly imaginary origins of their federation, the freedom and civilization now enjoyed by the Swiss could not have come into being, it might still be said that here, as in many other instances, undeniably good results have followed from actions largely determined by erroneous convictions held by those who performed them; and that the Swiss citizen of to-day is as fully justified in congratulating himself upon these good results as if his forefathers had not been the dupes of what Plato might have called a "noble lie"[1] respecting the origin of his nation. Yet, when all this is granted, can we seriously deny that a discovery of the falsity, not only of details, even where belief in these has been cherished, but of the substance of what has been taken as the past history of our own people would undermine a confidence which is at least comparable to that which each one of us places, and must place, in his own memory, the shaking of which must be as subversive of the stability of the public mentality as is the loss of individual memory of that of private? Neither memory nor tradition enjoys the privilege of infallibility; but a general reliance on the latter is as indispensable to the maintenance of corporate as is a general reliance on the former to that of individual personality. And I think

[1] *Rep.*, iii, 414B.

we may add that in neither case is it possible to lay down in advance the precise limits within which memory can be convicted of inaccuracy or tradition of unfaithfulness to fact without destroying the confidence necessary for what I have called the maintenance of personality. But, as it would not be difficult to suggest delusions about his past which we should consider incompatible with regarding as sane the man who suffered from them, so one may, I think, easily imagine a degree of error respecting the past of a community which could not be confessed as such compatibly with the preservation in its members of that sense of corporate identity which seems necessary to anything that can be called corporate personality.

The upshot of these remarks is that what I understand by the historical element in religion is the tradition of the past of a religious community which is associated in the minds of its members with their sense of sharing in its life.

But it may be said that if we define it in this manner we shall not be able to find any historical element in the type of religion which Professor Whitehead presumably had in mind when he spoke, in the well-known passage to which I have already referred,[1] of religion being "what the individual does with his own

[1] Above, p. 14.

solitariness"; in the religion of the mystic who, intent on union with the object of worship, flies, in the famous words of Plotinus, "alone to the Alone";[1] or, again, of the prophet who, in the silence of lonely prayer and meditation, hears the voice of God speaking directly to his soul.

In reply to this criticism I should be prepared to contend that, in principle, the "historical element" is not absent even from such religious experiences as these, in so far as the conception entertained of God by mystic or prophet is, as a matter of fact, in all cases affected, if not determined, by the tradition of the community in which he received his first religious impressions; but I do not here desire to insist upon this point. I shall hope, however, at a later stage of this course, to indicate the connexion which I believe exists between the sense of continuity with the past which is so intimately associated with much, if not with all, religious experience and that aspect of religion as essentially communion with God—or, as Baron von Hügel said, "adoration"—in which it might at first sight seem able to dispense with any such sense, as irrelevant to what is apparently experienced as actual intercourse with a Being immediately present to the worshipper. At present I will only conclude

---

[1] *Enn.*, VI, ix, 11.

this first Lecture with repeating once more the truth, as I take it to be, that the "historical element in religion" is primarily a sense of continuity with the past of the religious community of which a man finds or makes himself a member, and through which, at any rate for the most part, his religious experience is mediated. In my next Lecture I shall examine the importance assigned to this element in various religions, and especially in that which I myself, and probably most of those who will read this book, know best, namely, Christianity.

II

IN my first Lecture I endeavoured to clear the ground by attempting to assign a precise meaning to "the historical element in religion," and suggested that it is because religious experience is normally mediated to the individual through a community and is bound up with a sense of continuity with the past of that community that religion is found to involve such an element at all. If this be so, it is obvious that the interest of religion in history is primarily not a dispassionate interest in past events as such, but an interest in the past of a community of which one is conscious of being oneself a member and whose past one therefore appropriates, although one does not *remember* it as having formed part of one's own individual experience. I pass now to what I stated at the beginning of my former Lecture as the subject to be treated in my second, namely, the importance actually assigned in religion to the historical element as thus understood. This we shall find to vary greatly in different religions, and to be at its maximum in the religion with which most of us are best acquainted, namely, Christianity.

In an extremely interesting work which was recently

published by Mr. Michael Oakeshott, of Gonville and Caius College, Cambridge, *Experience and its Modes*,[1] to which I shall again have occasion to refer in the course of these Lectures, the author, speaking of History as a mode of experience, remarks that "the world lived long and happily enough before it appeared."[2] He is thinking here of History in the sense which that word bears on the lips of a modern scholar who regards as an irrelevant and disturbing element all *special* interest in the past of a community, religious or otherwise, to which we ourselves happen to belong, due to the fact that this past affects our practical life, though it be only to the extent of warming or chilling our affections towards the community whose past it is. It is indeed perfectly true that a dispassionate interest in the past, as such, is late in appearance and must always be rare. It is also very well that philosophers like Mr. Oakeshott should insist upon the fallacy involved in supposing the actual content of an experience to be wholly determined by its antecedents, psychological or otherwise. This fallacy is exemplified by the mistake—to which in my previous Lecture[3] I have already referred in another connexion—not infrequently made by writers on what is called "anthro-

[1] Cambridge, 1933.   [2] Page 350.
[3] Above, p. 12.

pology" in regarding the religious life of civilized men in the present as a mere "survival" of that observed among less civilized races in the present or described in the records of the past as existing at earlier stages of the development of human culture. The same fallacy is also, I believe, illustrated by the attempt which is sometimes made by psychologists and by philosophers who are content to seek in psychology for an explanation of principles which psychology, like every other science, must assume, to call in question the essential difference between knowledge and belief, and in so doing to ignore the significance of the pretension of the human mind to be capable of recognizing (though it be only by a refusal to endorse the claim of whatever offers itself as such) a *truth* not merely relative but absolute.

But, while I am in sympathy with Mr. Oakeshott's desire to emphasize this characteristic not of the historian's outlook only but of experience generally— a characteristic which is often overlooked and sometimes pertinaciously denied—I venture to think him mistaken in going to an opposite extreme from the position of those whom he is criticizing, and in declining as unphilosophical the problem of relating history, science, and practical life to one another and to philosophy otherwise than as modes of experience completely shut off each from each, without means of communication, like the windowless monads of Leibnitz. As I hope to make clear in a later Lecture, I remain quite unconvinced by the arguments which he brings in support of the view that to ask what concern religion has with history or, again, with ultimate truth, is merely to commit the fallacy of *ignoratio elenchi* and to prove oneself to be not yet even a beginner at the game of philosophy. But even Mr. Oakeshott would probably not deny that such an interest in the past as I have said is associated with religion as, normally, a communal experience has in fact (as I hinted in my last Lecture[1]) been an ante-cedent condition of the rise of that very dispassionate interest in the past as such to which alone he would allow the title of an interest in *history*, properly so called.

In any case it was already recognized by the Greek thinkers who founded the philosophical study of religion that a body of narratives purporting to relate past events did as a matter of fact form one kind of *theologia*, that is, of one kind of account of the objects of religious worship. St. Augustine has preserved for us in his great book, *de Civitate Dei*, some fragments of the *Antiquitates* of the Roman scholar Varro, in

[1] Above, p. 20.

which, following, as is supposed, Panaetius, a Stoic philosopher of the second century before Christ, he had given a classification of *genera theologiae* as *mythicon*, *physicon*, and *civile* respectively—legendary, natural, political—as we may perhaps English these words.[1] The first of these is used, Varro tells us, by priests, the second by philosophers, the third by statesmen. To Varro himself only the second, which we still call by the same name as he gives it, "Natural Theology," had any genuine truth in it. The stories which constitute the first or legendary kind, the rules of ritual observance which make up the third or political kind, can only be explained (he thinks) as more than mere fairy-tales in the one case, and as more than mere arbitrary customs in the other, by seeing in them figurative descriptions or dramatic representations of those real natural phenomena in which alone is revealed to the philosopher the only true God, the Soul of the World, by whose immanent reason the motions of the stars and elements are ordered and controlled. To Greek and Roman scholars these three kinds of *theologia* no doubt seemed more obviously distinct from one another than they were or are in more primitive societies than those to which they themselves belonged. Much of what they called

[1] Aug., *de Civitate Dei*, vi, 5.

the *genus mythicon theologiae* or *theologia fabulosa* had
no doubt originated in explanations of rites and
ceremonies in which the communal religious life
found expression and about which the elders would
wish to have an answer when their children asked,
"What mean you by this service?" These rites and
ceremonies again, though not, as Varro probably
supposed, deliberately invented to symbolize natural
phenomena regarded as such, were doubtless to a
great extent attempts to control such phenomena in
the interest of the community by the magical manipu-
lation of them through imitation or otherwise, or
sometimes by the propitiation of manlike beings
whose activity was supposed to have brought them
about. The discrepancy between the three kinds of
theology noted by the authors of the distinction is to
be explained by the fact that the understanding of
these natural phenomena then possessed by philosophers was vastly greater than that implied in the
traditional stories or in the traditional observances
which were still perpetuated in the songs of the poets
and in the customs of the State. Among the Greeks,
in particular, the growth of a great national literature
over against the peculiar cults of the local sanctuaries
had created a marked divergence between mythology
and ritual, a divergence still further emphasized

c

among the Romans by the circumstance that, when they came under the influence of Hellenic culture, their men of letters had introduced the luxuriant mythology created by the powerful imagination of their Greek neighbours to fill the place left vacant in their own religious system by the paucity of tales about their native *numina*, those vaguely imagined powers which presided over the various details of the Roman citizen's public and private life.

So long as we have to do with mere mythology, with tales told in explanation of a traditional ritual or in order to satisfy that curiosity about remarkable things and events which is characteristic of human nature, and is indeed the wonder wherein, according to Plato,[1] philosophy begins, we are hardly concerned with an historical element in religion in the sense in which the presence of such an element constitutes a serious problem for the philosophy of religion. Such tales may often, of course, have in fact preserved a tradition of real events; but so long as they are told only as having happened "once upon a time"; so long as the important thing was (as, for the most part, even in ancient Greece) that the ritual should be correctly performed—that, as Burnet puts it,[2] the worshipper

---

[1] *Theaet.*, 155D. Cp. Ar., *Met.*, A. 982b, 12.
[2] *Early Greek Philosophy*, p. 91.

should duly sacrifice his pig—and it was considered on the whole a matter of indifference what explanation he gave of the meaning of his act; so long we cannot dignify the tales with the name of history, nor is faith in them as a true account of past occurrences reckoned to be an essential part of religion.

When dates are assigned to the occurrence of the events related in the tales, and an attempt is made to synchronize them with events related in the tales handed down by others, we have the beginnings of history in the proper sense; but this history only becomes an element in religion when belief in it comes to be regarded as the justification for the ritual act the institution of which it is invoked to explain. To describe in detail the place occupied in the various great religions which have claimed the allegiance of civilized men by the record of the past of the communities which profess them would be a task which neither my knowledge nor the time at my disposal permits me to attempt; I shall therefore in the present Lecture confine myself in the main from this point onward to the historical element in Christianity, touching only incidentally, by way of illustration, comparison, or contrast, on the historical element in other religions. This course, however, may be defended not only on the ground of the special interest of this religion to myself and most of my readers, but also by the notorious fact that in no other religion has so great an importance been attributed to belief in the authorized account of its origin; so that in dealing with the historical element in Christianity one is dealing with the problem of the historical element in religion in its acutest form. If the claims made for it here can be substantiated, the inferior claims made for it elsewhere will be covered by these; if, on the other hand, they are dismissed, there is no religion on which such dismissal will have an effect comparable with its effect on Christianity.

The peculiar importance which has generally been attached to the historical element in Christianity is connected with three characteristic features of that religion, two of which it shares with other systems, while in respect of one of them it stands alone among the principal faiths which challenge the allegiance of civilized men to-day. The first feature is the possession of a sacred book which is believed to be inspired to reveal the nature and will of the God who is proposed as the object of worship. The second feature is the conception of that God as a transcendent Being communicating his will through the medium of prophets to whom he speaks directly and of a community to which is entrusted the message thus received. The third is the divine dignity attributed to its Founder. I will say something of each of these features in turn.

The Christian Bible is of course by no means the only book or collection of books for which divine authority is claimed. Similar pretensions are put forward for the Vedas, for the Koran, for that oldest part of itself which is acknowledged by Jews as well as by Christians. But of neither Vedas nor Koran does a narrative purporting to be a record of past facts form so large a proportion as it does of the Christian Bible, nor does the tradition either of Hinduism or of Islam, exalted as are the terms in which the dignity of their respective Scriptures are expressed, assign to the events described therein the unique significance and religious value which Jews and Christians have been wont to attribute to those related in the Bible. Such an estimate of any temporal occurrence would run directly counter to the genius of Hinduism, with its alternating cycles of creation and destruction and its tendency to see in the multiplicity of phenomena only the infinite variety of masks assumed by the One eternal Actor. According to this way of thinking, the religious value of a particular historical event, personality, or institution can hardly be unique or exclude the possibility of alternatives better suited to other contexts. In contrast to Hinduism, Islam belongs, along with Zoroastrianism,

Judaism, and Christianity, to what we may call the prophetic group of religions; and a unique significance within a single historical process is certainly attributed to the mission of Mohammed. But the Koran is only incidentally concerned with the Prophet's biography or with that of the earlier messengers of God whom he recognized as having preceded him in announcing the divine judgments; it is essentially a record of the contents of the communications made to the Prophet on the part of God; only so far as we are told the circumstances in which they were made, or so far as former revelations are adduced by way of illustration, does narrative enter into it at all.

But when we come to the Old Testament we find quite a different state of things. There are here, no doubt, as in the Vedas, ritual laws and hymns of praise; as in the Koran, divine threatenings and promises communicated through chosen messengers; but a great part of the whole is devoted to the history of Israel, conceived of as a record of God's dealings with his people, and it can, I think, be said with truth that this is the framework within which are set the rules of conduct, the songs of triumph and of penitence, the prophetic anticipations of judgment or of glory that are also to be found there. There are, no doubt, certain portions of the collection, such as the

Proverbs and Ecclesiastes, the Song of Songs, and the Book of Job, which have no direct or obvious reference to this setting; but of the greater part of it it may certainly be affirmed that it has one theme running through it, and that this is the theme of the love borne by Jahveh, the God of Israel, amid all the vicissitudes due to the waywardness of Israel's response, toward the nation which alone of all the families of the earth he had chosen to be his peculiar inheritance.

It is important here to bear in mind that this history is presented in the canonical books not as the history of Israel alone, but as that of mankind, though no doubt with Israel in the centre of the picture; and Jahveh himself as not merely the God of Israel, but as the only real God, the creator of heaven and earth and the ruler of all mankind, who had, according to the prophet Amos, brought up the Philistines from Caphtor and the Syrians from Kir no less than Israel out of the land of Egypt.[1] In this way, however Israel's own national traditions may have been uncritically taken as a sufficient authority for statements regarding the past not of Israel only but of other peoples, the "historical element" in the Old Testament is already, in intention and profession, not a mere collection of stories, but a history of the world, although no doubt

[1] Amos ix. 7.

a history of the world told from a special point of view and with a practical intent. Moreover, it may be said to possess a truly religious significance in that what is narrated is designed to evoke the reader's faith and trust in him whose power and trustworthiness is so strongly attested by the narrative of his deeds in the time of old.

In this respect the New Testament is true to the type of the Old. The narratives of the life of Jesus, and especially of his passion, death, and resurrection, followed by those of the adventures of St. Paul and other apostles in preaching the Gospel, carry on the tradition of the older Scriptures. They concentrate the reader's attention on what is taken to be God's crowning visitation of his people; while even those letters of St. Paul and other early teachers of the Christian Church which constitute a considerable part of the whole book are principally devoted to emphasizing the momentous significance of the historical events recorded in the narrative with which they are conjoined.

The New Testament, however, does not merely carry on the tradition of the Old in the importance belonging to the historical element in its composition. This importance is immensely heightened by the exalted view taken by its writers of the person of their

Master. As the Son of God in a unique sense and declared to be such by his resurrection from the dead, he is not in the position of a prophet who derives his significance from what he says and does; rather his acts and words derive their significance from what he *is*; and this is what none other than he can be. But I am anticipating what I have to say of the third feature which I noted as characteristic of Christianity and as affecting the relative importance of the historical element in it; and I must first say something of the second, which, it will be remembered, was the conception of God as a transcendent Being revealing himself through prophets who communicate to others what they have received from him. This conception, like the possession of a sacred book, is of course by no means peculiar to Christianity. It is found also not only in the sister religion of Judaism, but in Zoroastrianism and in Mohammedanism; and it distinguishes this group of faiths from those to which Hinduism belongs, wherein God is thought of rather as the true Self of all, the consciousness of distinction from whom it is the aim of a religious man's ambition to lose, than as a Being essentially other and higher than we, *communion* but not *union* with whom is the goal of his worshipper's aspiration. To the same group with Hinduism belongs Buddhism; for here too the aim is to lose the consciousness of separate existence, although this goal is described otherwise than in Hinduism. What here concerns us with respect to the last-mentioned feature of Christianity is its relation to the emphasis laid upon the historical element in that religion. It is, I think, obvious that, where the prevailing religious temper is that which would be generally understood by the term "mystical," where what the worshipper has mainly in view is immediate union with the object of worship rather than a communion rendered possible by a revelation mediated through inspired prophets, there the record of the religious experiences of others in the past may indeed excite sympathetic interest, but will have far less importance for the religious life than where the record is regarded as the guarantee of the revelation which is presupposed as the condition of communion with the God who is revealed. To say this is not to suggest either that the mystic's conception of the Being with whom he seeks to be made one is independent of the community in which he has been bred, or that conscious dependence on a revelation which took place in the past excludes the possibility of a mystical experience of union with the God who has thus been revealed. The very existence of great Christian mystics is a proof that such experience is possible under these conditions. But it remains true that in what we may call by way of distinction the prophetic type of religion, history, in the sense of the record of the past of the religious community to which one belongs, inevitably possesses a greater relative importance than belongs to it where all temporal process is treated as mere appearance or even as illusion, and where the quest of the religious devotee is directed rather to that which he himself essentially *is* than to what is primarily presented as, in Dr. Rudolf Otto's phrase, "wholly other"[1] than he, challenging him, as it were, from without; in the presence of whose majesty he, like Job, "abhors himself and repents in dust and ashes."[2]

But while Christianity shares the interest in the past which must be aroused wherever a religion commends to its adherents a sacred Scripture concerned with the past relations of their God to his worshippers and wherever access to that God is held to be conditioned by his revelation of himself to the founders, leaders, or prophets of the community in the past, the importance of the record of such a revelation must be vastly augmented by the third feature of Christianity, which I described as peculiar to it, namely, its doctrine of the Godhead of its Founder. I will not now do more than indicate the grounds on which I do not hesitate

[1] *Ganz andere.*   [2] Job xlii. 6.

to say that this doctrine is peculiar to Christianity. To hold that the founder of one's religion is *a* god is of course common enough. But in Christianity the historical Founder is regarded not as *a* god but as God in the strict sense which the word bears to a monotheist, nay, to a Jewish monotheist, the first article of whose faith is "Thy God is One" and the first commandment of his code the precept to have no gods beside that One. If we look aside for a moment to the other great religions which can be compared with Christianity, we shall see that here it stands alone. Hinduism is boundlessly hospitable in admitting the divinity of great teachers and leaders; but there is no limit to the possible number of those who may thus be honoured. No doubt it is held by Hindu theologians that they are all manifestations of One ultimate real Being; but this pantheistic doctrine of incarnation in an indefinite number of apparently distinct individuals is wholly different from that of the Christian, to whom there can be but one Incarnate Son of God, and He the historical Founder and Lord of the Christian society. Insistence on this uniqueness of Christ's divine sonship was, I think one may confidently say, characteristic of Christianity from the first, although no doubt neither in the New Testament nor for long after New Testament times was it expressed in the

terms which were ultimately devised to protect it
from any confusion with that deification of great and
good men which was common in the ancient Roman
Empire (as it has been common in modern India),
while at the same time keeping intact, as the foundation of the Christian creed, Israel's profession of faith
in the divine unity. And this divine unity, it must be
borne in mind, is that of a transcendent Creator of
heaven and earth and all that therein is, not of an
immanent Soul of the World, having nature in its
infinite multiplicity for his body. To the claim of
Godhead which is made by Christianity for its Founder
there is, I believe, no genuine parallel. To two founders
of religions claiming to be universal have no doubt
been rendered honours which may in a loose way of
speaking be called divine—to Mohammed and to
Gautama the Buddha. But to orthodox Mohammedanism the unity and incommunicableness of the
Godhead is as fundamental as to Judaism, and
Mohammed is never admitted within that unity. For
many Buddhists there is no doubt no higher being in
the universe than the Tatha'gata, the Perfectly En-
lightened One; but he is not God, for in Buddhism
proper there is no God. (I do not speak of what is
called Amida-Buddhism, where the highest Buddha is
no doubt truly God, but, on the other hand, is not

identified with the historical founder of Buddhism.)
Gods, indeed, supernatural beings such as those wor-
shipped by the Buddha's Indian fellow-countrymen,
are in the Buddhist scriptures admitted to exist; but
a Buddha is superior to these. On the other hand, to
be a Buddha is not a privilege reserved for Gautama
alone. That supreme spiritual dignity to which he
attained is not in principle unobtainable by others,
though it may only be after many successive lives;
and in Mahayana Buddhism it is actually held that
there were many Buddhas before Gautama, and the
Buddha-next-to-be receives worship along with the
historical figure of the great Teacher, who is, up to
the present time, the last to reach enlightenment.

Thus the homage rendered to the Founder of
Buddhism, however profound it may be, is of a different
character from that rendered by Christians to Jesus
precisely in those respects in which the latter has
tended so greatly to magnify the importance of the
historical element in Christianity. The Buddhahood
of Gautama is not regarded as uniquely his, as Jesus
is held by Christians to be the only Son of God;
Son of God, that is, in a sense in which none other
than he can be so described. The denial of the sub-
stantiality of the soul in the philosophy of Buddhism
and the readiness of Buddhist imagination to indulge

in speculation on incalculable periods of cosmical destruction and renovation alike mark the difference of the genius of Buddhism from that of Christianity with its emphasis upon the unique individuality of every human being within a single historic process, moving under providential guidance, from the creation to the consummation of all things. In view of this emphasis, and of the monotheism which Christianity inherits from the religion of Israel, the Christian worship of Jesus has a character quite other than the Buddhist veneration of Gautama, and confers upon the record of the Redeemer's life and work—the historical element in Christianity—an importance which is not claimed for the corresponding element in Buddhism, or indeed in any other creed.

I hope I have made clear not only this point, of the truth of which it needs no long exposition to convince any tolerably attentive observer of the facts—that in no religion is a greater importance attributed to the historical element than in Christianity—but also the intimate connexion which exists between the peculiar prominence of this element in Christianity and the characteristic features of its outlook on God and on the world. For Christianity God has manifested himself in history, and it is faith in God so manifested that is the moving spring of the life which it claims to be able to inspire in its adherents—a life of co-operation with God in the promotion of his kingdom of righteousness and love, both in the hearts of men and in the affairs of the world. In Christianity the historical element becomes even more important than in Judaism, precisely because of its distinguishing doctrine of the Incarnation. For, according to this doctrine, the revelation in the history of the chosen nation culminates in a revelation whose medium is the character and life of an individual person, whose death and resurrection are the grounds of the individual Christian's hopes of forgiveness and eternal life, by association of himself, through faith and sacraments, with this human mediator between God and man. The death and resurrection of this person and the life which was the prelude thereto become thus not mere exemplifications of timeless realities (though it must not be forgotten that even in the New Testament there are instances of their being thus interpreted, as when we read of the Lamb slain from the foundation of the world[1]), but the actual vehicles of the divine presence and certificates to Christians of their power to recognize it and to count upon it.

Now it is a patent fact that, within quite recent times—indeed, in the lifetime of the older among

[1] Rev. xiii. 3.

ourselves—a revolution has taken place in the attitude of Christian scholars toward the writings which contain the narratives of those events to which Christians attach so high an importance—a revolution which, we may be well assured, cannot be without far-reaching consequences for our estimate of the importance of the historical element in Christianity. The application to the Bible of the critical principles which are universally applied to all other ancient literatures; our vastly increased knowledge of the circumstances in which it took shape and our acquaintance, due to the comparative study of religion, with the numerous parallels and analogies to be found in the traditions of other peoples to the stories, the institutions, and the doctrines contained in our own Scriptures—all these have profoundly modified the views commonly entertained of these sacred writings even by those whose acquaintance with the reasons for the change is superficial and second-hand. We have here to notice that what has happened is that the rise of a new ideal of historical knowledge has, by casting doubt upon the historical value of the traditional account of the origins of the Christian faith and life—which constituted the historical element in Christianity—raised in an acute form the question of the importance to that faith and life of this historical element. In the primitive age of

D

Christianity the belief that the Lord and Saviour whom it proclaimed was a real historical person, who had lived and died within comparatively recent times, gave it an undoubted advantage over such a rival faith as Mithraism, which could only offer as its divine hero a figure belonging to mythical antiquity, to whose exploits no date could be assigned, and who could be identified with the Sun in the sky. All down the centuries since, though the authenticity of details in the record might be doubted, the existence of an historical tradition which was not only accepted without demur in uncritical ages, but the soundness of which could in more learned times be maintained by scholars with solid arguments, was certainly a source of strength to the religion of Christ. We face a new situation when a sense of insecurity in all traditional beliefs about the past, due to the destructive results of a new criticism, at once more scrupulous in its estimate of evidence and more imaginative in its recognition of the psychological diversity to be expected between men belonging to different periods of intellectual and cultural development, has led to serious doubt whether Christianity is not at a disadvantage in consequence of the stress commonly laid by its defenders upon the historical element in its doctrine, as compared with faiths which, attaching less weight to that element, are less exposed to disturbance by the vicissitudes of scholarly opinion. We are thus brought to the consideration of views depreciating the importance of the historical element in religion. This is the topic to which I propose to devote my third Lecture.

III

THE present Lecture will be devoted to the depreciation by certain thinkers of the importance of the historical element in religion. Such depreciation may be due to the desire, mentioned at the end of my previous Lecture, to remove religion from exposure to the changes and chances of historical criticism; or it may be consequential upon views of the nature of history which tend to create a divergence in principle between the presuppositions of history and those of religion, and so to render illegitimate any attempt to combine the ways of looking at the world which are characteristic of the historian and of the religious man respectively.

The development within the last two centuries of what may be called the historical sense, and the increase of historical knowledge which has been in part the cause and in part the effect of this development, have, no doubt, by unsettling the confidence of Christians (for it is among peoples professing Christianity that these processes have chiefly taken place) in the records of the origin of their faith, promoted an inclination among the more thoughtful to minimize the importance of history to religion. But, before either the development of an historical sense or the progress of historical knowledge had gone very far, a great philosopher had already anticipated the outcome of the development and that progress by devoting one of his most remarkable works to the disentanglement of theology from the beliefs about history traditionally associated therewith. I am, as my readers will surmise, referring to the *Tractatus Theologico-Politicus* of Spinoza. It would be an error to suppose that the position adopted in that famous book in regard to the historical element in religion in general—particularly in Judaism, the writer's original religion, and in Christianity, the religion established in his country of domicile—was wholly without precedent. On the contrary, in essentials it had been assumed in the period of the Renaissance by such thinkers as, for example, Pomponazzi, but in a setting less modern than that in which it is presented by Spinoza, whose background is here, as usual, the Cartesian philosophy, with its emphasis on the clearness and distinctness of ideas as the certificate of their conformity to reality. Neither belief in the election by God of a particular nation to enjoy his favour, which is the dominant theme of the Old Testament narrative, nor yet belief in the truth of the accounts of miracles reported in the New Testament as having attended and followed the ministry of Christ, is compatible, according to

Spinoza, with that true knowledge of God which is equivalent to a full comprehension of the absolute necessity and reciprocal determination of every part of that all-embracing system which may be indifferently called either Nature or God. Nor does he consider these beliefs to be reconcilable with our practical interests, for these require only the belief that God, being himself just and good, approves those qualities and enjoins those actions which conduce to human well-being. It must indeed be added that this latter belief is, in Spinoza's judgment, practical rather than scientific; for, according to him, God, strictly speaking, has neither understanding nor will in the sense in which these words are used when we talk of them as belonging to human beings. It is clear that, on Spinoza's principles, no importance can be attached to the historical element in religion except, at the most, that of calling attention to teaching, the intrinsic value of which is independent of the historical circumstances of its utterance. Even if Christ, for instance, was, as Spinoza in one place seems prepared to admit, unique in the truth and adequacy of his notions—in their objectivity (to use a term which is, in this sense, of more recent use)—so that he is, as Spinoza expresses it, "rather the mouth than the prophet of God,"[1] yet

[1] *Tract. Theol.-Polit.*, c. 4, § 31.

we cannot, consistently with the general principles laid down by this philosopher, regard belief in this or any other fact as forming part of that rule of life which, when apprehended by the "light of nature," is able, altogether apart from acquaintance with any historical narrative whatsoever, to make men blessed or happy. Thus Spinoza's rejection of the historical element in religion as a permanent feature thereof is, in the end, uncompromising and complete. But, if we go on to ask what is left of religion after this thorough-going elimination of the historical element, it is far less easy to be confident what one's answer should be. At first sight one may be tempted to reply: "Morality and the vision of God." Certainly, if these are left, it would seem that nothing was lost but "anise and cummin" and that the pearl of great price was left intact. I doubt, however, whether this answer will bear a close inspection. The pure and disinterested character of Spinoza himself and the lofty solemnity of the passage respecting the disinterested love of God in which his *Ethics* culminates incline one to assume, perhaps too readily, that our moral consciousness was to him, as it was to Kant, the supreme revelation of God, and that his God, whom he would have us love without thought of any reciprocation of our love, is the object of the devotion of Hebrew psalmist or Christian saint at

their highest and best. But I must confess that the
study of the actual teaching of Spinoza tends to make
me doubtful whether these assumptions are correct.
I must content myself now with the statement that I
find myself led to see in Spinoza's life, and in the
religious note which he strikes when he is attempting
to describe the goal of our intellectual ambition, not so
much the fruit of his own distinctive philosophy, but
of the piety of his own people, that people which has
been, in the words of Athanasius,[1] the school of the
knowledge of God to all the world, with its characteristic passion for the law of God and its profound
sense of the presence of One who is not only the
Beloved but the Lover of souls,[2] not only the high
and lofty inhabitant of eternity but One who shares
the high and holy place with him that is of a con-
trite and humble spirit.[3] I cannot find in Spinoza's
declared view of the relation of God to morality or
in his conception of the universal system which he
calls God, anything which, apart from the influence, surviving in his soul, of the faith which he
had inherited but abandoned, can justify either a
religious view of morality or a religious attitude
toward God.

[1] *De Incarnatione Verbi*, c. 12, § 5.
[2] Wisd. xi. 26.   [3] Isa. lvii. 15.

When Spinoza wrote, biblical criticism, which since his day has so profoundly affected the attitude of Christian scholars toward the classical records of the divine revelation which they, as Christians, believe themselves to have received, was still only in its infancy. It is, however, worthy of remark that the *Tractatus Theologico-Politicus* itself is distinguished by some acute remarks, which anticipate later comments on the sacred text, and especially by a passage[1] in which he brings together the wonderful exploits attributed by Ariosto to his Orlando, those related by Ovid concerning Perseus, and those to be found in the Old Testament stories of Samson and Elijah, in order to point the lesson, which has since received so much illustration and reinforcement from the comparative study of religion, that the Scriptural narratives must not be exempted from the operation of those general principles of criticism which are assumed to be applicable to all other literature.

But when we come to Lessing, a century later—a thinker who, we may note, was among the first to rehabilitate the credit of Spinoza as a master of spiritual philosophy after a period in which he had been regarded as the prince of atheists and mentioned, even by so liberal-minded a philosopher as Locke, as

[1] c. 7, §§ 61, 62.

on that account "justly decried"[1]—when, I say, we come to Lessing, we find the critical study of the New Testament narratives well launched. Lessing himself published anonymously the famous "Wolfen-büttel fragments" of Reimarus, with whom Dr. Albert Schweitzer begins his celebrated record of that study, known in the English version as *The Quest of the Historical Jesus*. For Lessing the historical element has only a pedagogic value. When the eternal truths concerning God's nature and our relation to him have come to be apprehended as matter of rational conviction, the promise of the "new covenant" will have been fulfilled, and the Scriptures that have played so great a part in that "education of the human race" which gave a title to one of his best-known works will have accomplished their task, and our posterity will be able henceforth to dispense with them. In Kant's *Religion within the Limits of Reason Alone* the great philosopher in whom the so-called *Aufklarung*, this Illumination or Enlightenment of the seventeenth and eighteenth centuries, reached its climax and the way was prepared for the new direction of thought, inspired by the idea of development or evolution, which was to characterize the nineteenth century, sets

[1] *Reply to the Bishop of Worcester and Answer to his Second Letter* (1699), p. 422.

forth a view of the historical element in religion which is in principle the same as Lessing's. From Spinoza's it differs chiefly in one point—but that a very important point: I refer to the fact, which I have already mentioned, that the moral truths in the communication and illustration of which consists, according to both philosophers, the true use and value of the sacred history, are regarded by Kant, as they are *not* regarded by Spinoza, as a more genuine revelation of the nature of God than is to be looked for from any exercise of the purely theoretical reason.

By Hegel, in the generation after Kant's, history may be said to have been raised to a status in philosophy which it had not possessed in the eyes of his predecessors. For Kant, whatever foreshadowings of later speculation on this subject may be found in his writings, the philosophical importance of history was, on the whole, no more than that of an illustration of truths independently apprehended by the reason. If the narratives contained in the Scriptures of Christianity are to be preferred to those of other religions, it is only because they are found to be better adapted to suggest and commend such truths to the attention of mankind. There does not seem to be any reason why some other narratives might not be discovered which would surpass them in this respect, as they themselves surpass those already known to us beside. Nor is the historical accuracy of their statements a matter of any religious importance, since there can be no moral value in the knowledge of a fact as such, though there may well be great moral value in the attitude toward life of which such a fact may serve as a suggestive symbol. To Hegel, on the other hand, the history through which the Idea, the spiritual Reality, has in fact revealed itself is no mere accident. The stages in the development of the process of its revelation are factors in its being which are necessary to the "result" which it is. This way of looking at history obviously imparts to it a philosophical significance which it has not for such a thinker as Kant; and it plainly goes some way towards justifying the veneration felt by Christians for the sacred history of the origin of their religion. For from this point of view that history is more than a symbol of eternal truths apprehended by the reason; it is the actual, nay, since in the end what is real is rational, it is the necessary process of their self-disclosure.

But there is another side to this contrast between Hegel and Kant, and between the types of philosophy associated with these two great names respectively. Against the general depreciation of all history by the Kantian philosophy is to be set the emphasis laid by

Kant upon the divergence between what *is* and what *ought to be*; a divergence which could, in his view, only be overcome by an act of faith, itself based upon the native aspiration of the reason after an ultimate unity of all reality, in a God whose power is equal to the goodness of his will. Although the authority of Kant cannot be claimed for the suggestion, it has been found possible to hold, against the background of this doctrine of the reconciliation in God of the ideal and the real, that the historical revelation which Christians believe to have been made in the life, death, and resurrection of the Founder of their religion was, so to say, an anticipatory manifestation of that sovereignty of the ethical ideal over the course of the world which, according to Kant, reason was constrained to divine and even to postulate as the ground of conduct. In other words, a philosophy which depreciated the importance of the sacred history as such, and considered it only as symbolical of eternal moral truths, yet, by admitting the transcendence of what *is* by what *ought to be*, left room for the thought of the revelation of an order other than that explored by the natural sciences, a revelation of which historical events might be the medium. On the other hand, the later philosophy which saw disclosed in history the very structure of the eternal reality, by its affirmation of the immanence of that reality, not in *certain* historical facts but in *all*, while it allowed to history, as such, a higher value than had been allowed to it by Kant, at the same time cut away the ground from the prerogative importance attached by Christian tradition to a certain particular history as the witness to a transcendent order and the vehicle of its revelation.

Now here we have to do with a tendency which —in very various forms—dominated the philosophy of religion throughout the nineteenth century: I mean the tendency to find the religious values not, as had previously been the case, in *another* world than this, represented in this world only by institutions, the Church or the Scripture, which could be regarded as the vehicles of a revelation from that other world, but *within* this world, and even within that civilization which the older view had been apt to disparage as merely secular or profane. This tendency, which may be conveniently designated as "immanentism," has in the present generation culminated in the work of Croce, who boasts that he has stripped philosophy of those rags of "transcendence" which were left to her by Hegel, and has left no world of ideas to be contrasted with the historical facts in which they are immanent, no God other than the God which is in us and which we are, *Deus in nobis et nos.* For him, religion, which those (so he tells us[1]) who are outside its magic circle call by its proper name of mythology, is just an infantile essay in philosophy, by which men attempt to understand the real world (which is that of history) by setting over against it its own meaning and value as though it were *another* real world, in which there dwells a God who has already determined the course of history before it began and who is to pass judgment upon it after it is over and done with. In Croce's view, philosophy does but reproduce this type of sham explanation in a form less crudely mythological when (with Plato) it duplicates the real world by inventing an ideal world of values to which it either ought to conform or (as Hegel teaches) does in reality conform. Thus, according to the Italian philosopher, there is no historical element in religion; there is only a religious misinterpretation of history. The narratives traditionally associated with religion are not history in any true sense, and, when they are not merely fictitious, can only be transformed into history by putting off their religious character. Nevertheless, since religion is, for Croce, a crude attempt to philosophize, that is, to understand history, the presence in a religion of what passes for an historical element may perhaps be regarded, in accordance with

[1] *Teoria e Storia della Storiografia*, p. 51.

his principles, as implicitly an anticipation of the truth on which he is concerned to insist, that philosophy is not to be regarded as something wholly other than history, removed (as it is in religions which lack or set little store by an historical element) to some "regions mild of calm and serene air, Above the smoke and stir of this dim spot Which men call earth,"[1] but rather as immanent in history itself. In this way the Crocean criticism of religion may be regarded as allowing to the professedly historical religions a certain superiority over the frankly unhistorical.

If, however, we turn from Croce to a younger thinker among our contemporaries, to whom I referred in a previous Lecture, Mr. Oakeshott, we shall meet with a more thorough-going refusal than is made by any of those whom I have so far noticed, with the exception of Spinoza, to allow that any legitimate place can be found for an "historical element" in religion. " 'God in history,' " says Mr. Oakeshott,[2] "is . . . a contradiction, a meaningless phrase. Wherever God is, he is not in history, for, if he were, there would no longer be any history. 'God in history' indicates an incursion of the practical past into the historical past, an incursion which brings only chaos." It is obvious

[1] Milton, *Comus*, 4–6.
[2] *Experience and its Modes*, p. 127.

that these trenchant expressions convey a complete rejection of what is, at any rate at first sight, a distinctive feature of Christianity. This Mr. Oakeshott appears to admit when in a previous chapter of his book to that from which my last quotation was taken, he says,[1] speaking of the Hebrews: "The past had meaning for them only so far as it was their own past. . . . They did not, of course, think of this past as a merely fancied past; its power to capture the imagination was due entirely to the fact that it was believed to be a past which had actually happened. But this belief," continues Mr. Oakeshott, "cannot of itself convert what is essentially a practical past into an historical past: it is merely part of the paraphernalia required to extract from the past the inspiration and the life which practical experience seeks. This Hebrew dependence upon the past," he adds, "was taken over by Christianity, and has now become embedded in our religion."

The uncompromising thoroughness of Mr. Oakeshott's criticism of any claim on the part of religion to include an historical element properly so called, and the ability and lucidity with which this criticism is expounded, render it very suitable for our consideration here. It would be, I venture to think,

[1] *Experience and its Modes*, p. 104.

E

difficult to find any better means of clarifying our thoughts regarding the true character of such a claim than the putting to ourselves of the question: What are Mr. Oakeshott's reasons for repudiating it? And how far, if at all, can these reasons be rebutted?

For Mr. Oakeshott, "philosophy" is simply experience carried out to the bitter end. History, and also practice, of which he regards religion as merely the highest kind—not to mention Science, with which we are not for the moment concerned—are what he calls "arrests of experience" and designates as "modes" of experience. History, or historical experience, is the world envisaged *sub specie praeteritorum*;[1] practice, or practical experience, is the same world envisaged *sub specie voluntatis*.[2] There is no contact between these different "modes"; there is a great gulf fixed between them, and we cannot pass from one to the other except by committing the fallacy of *ignoratio elenchi* or irrelevance. What is still more surprising is that these "modes" of experience have no contact with the complete experience which is philosophy: they make no contribution to it, nor has it anything, whether by way of criticism or otherwise, to say to them. To suppose that the philosopher should, as in the famous

[1] *Experience and its Modes*, p. 111.
[2] Ibid., p. 258.

parable in Plato's *Republic*,[1] return from his contemplation of ultimate reality to the care of practical life, better equipped for kingship there by his enjoyment of the heavenly vision—this was, in Mr. Oakeshott's opinion,[2] a fatal mistake on the part of Plato. The individual man who is a philosopher may—indeed, if he is to live at all, *must*—return thither; but he will have gained nothing of value for practical life by his commerce with the very truth. In that commerce he will indeed have found while it lasted, what nothing else could have afforded him, a secure refuge from the essentially unanswerable questions (as of the resemblance of a Raven to a Writing-desk) suggested by history or science or practice to minds which venture to peep outside the predestined limits of these worlds and venture to enquire what relations these may have to other sorts of experience, which force themselves on the attention of all but the most bigoted devotees of that which is their main concern.

I can of course at present only in the briefest possible fashion indicate where Mr. Oakeshott's account of the matter appears to me to be unsatisfactory. I hope that those who may be interested by what I have just been saying will compare my remarks

[1] *Rep.*, vii, 539 E.
[2] *Experience and its Modes*, pp. 303, 320. Cp. p. 355.

with the book to which they relate. In making that book my text I am attempting to repay to the best of my ability the debt which I feel that I owe to its author for the great assistance which the perusal of his work has afforded me in arranging and putting to the question my thoughts upon the subject with which I am dealing in this course of Lectures.

"God in history" is necessarily to Mr. Oakeshott "a meaningless phrase" because the word "God" to him means one of two things. It may, as in the language of some philosophers, mean the universal system of reality which is the presupposition of all events, and to which therefore no one event can be attributed any more than any other; or it may, as in the common language of mankind, be the name of a "practical idea" which, though it may be the master inspiration of our lives, can be of no possible service either to the philosopher or to the historian; while "history," in its turn, signifies to Mr. Oakeshott simply the world of past events as such, abstracted from any consideration either of their causes or of their value. Perhaps, when this is understood, the sweeping pronouncement which I have quoted from his book will come to seem to us less startling than at first; and after the intimidating effects of his dogmatic tone have worn off, we may begin again to mutter some of those questions from which he has sternly warned us off as merely irrelevant. Is that experience truly complete (so we may venture to enquire) which is wholly out of contact with practical life, with history, and with science? Can religion without self-contradiction disinterest itself in ultimate truth? What are we to say of that unity of the personal soul or spirit, whereof philosophy, history, and science are themselves activities?

No doubt practical life, the historian's study of the past, and the scientific man's study of nature can be carried on without raising those questions about ultimate reality the discussion of which is the special business of philosophy. It is even true to say that the raising of those questions in the midst of an historical or scientific investigation, or, again, of the practical business of life—as though one could not pursue these till those questions were solved—would often or always result in nothing but distraction and confusion. But it is surely one thing to admit this and quite another to deny to religion any lawful interest in the ultimate truth of its ideas. I will allow that the historian, as such, and the man of science, as such—although I cannot feel content to hold with Mr. Oakeshott that neither history nor science has any contribution to make to philosophy—are not interested in criticizing, as the philosopher must criticize, the assumptions necessarily made by their respective studies. It is not without reason that they are apt to resent the impertinence of those who would puzzle them with such criticism. The practical man, likewise, is impatient, and rightly impatient, if asked to suspend all action till the philosophers have laid to rest their doubts about the value and meaning of life. But if religion, at any rate in its higher forms, is to be any part of life at all, it cannot possibly share this indifference to philosophy. Mr. Oakeshott himself really confesses as much when he darkly hints in one place[1] that too much curiosity about the attitude of philosophy toward the convictions by which religion lives is only too likely to issue in the discovery that this attitude is and must be hostile. That the form in which religion expresses these convictions is imaginative and symbolical, rather than satisfactory to the critical metaphysician, would, I suppose, be granted on all hands. There are few among those who trouble themselves about the matter—and Mr. Oakeshott's master, Mr. Bradley, was certainly not one of the few—but would acknowledge that the absence from the best philosophical account of experience attainable of much that we most prize in experience, but apprehend by other forms of consciousness than the

[1] *Experience and its Modes,* p. 310.

speculative understanding, constitutes a serious em-
barrassment to any claim that may be set up for
philosophy to be the complete and perfect form of
experience. Mr. Oakeshott himself is driven in the end
to cry,[1] "*Pereat veritas, fiat vita.*" But can we call that
"the truth" with which the facts of life are necessarily
inconsistent and on which we must turn our back if we
are not to find ourselves incapable of living? This
would be indeed to make of philosophy a *meditatio
mortis*[2] in another sense than Plato intended, and one
which Plato (as Mr. Oakeshott is aware) would
emphatically have repudiated. I cannot myself accept
a view which to my mind contradicts the very nature
of religion; and this because it misses the essence of
religion as the form of experience in which we are
aware of ultimate reality as intimately present to and
in ourselves; or, to put it another way, of ourselves
as belonging to or in touch with that which is ultimately real. This is, I believe, as true of what I have
called, in an earlier Lecture, the mystical type of
religious experience as of that which I called the
prophetic. In the last resort our consciousness of ourselves and our consciousness of God are bound up
together, and the philosophy for which God is not

[1] *Experience and its Modes*, p. 320.
[2] Ibid., p. 310 *n*.

ultimately real will find the self, which must ever be in fact our standard of reality, a mystery and an enigma. This it certainly is for Mr. Oakeshott and, I think, also (under the name of "finite centre of experience"[1]) for his master Mr. Bradley.

In my concluding Lecture I shall endeavour to suggest that the true importance of what is called the historical element in religion will be found to lie in the very fact which leads Mr. Oakeshott to condemn any mention of such a thing as mere irrelevance, due to lack of philosophical insight; namely, in its witness to a unity of philosophy, history, and practice, which he would deny to be possible or desirable.

[1] E.g. *Appearance and Reality*, p. 226.

IV

IN this, the last Lecture of my course, I propose, in the light of what has gone before—of the attempt in the first Lecture to define the nature of the historical element in religion; of the survey in the second of the position assigned to it in Christianity; and of the depreciation of its importance on various grounds by the thinkers discussed in the third—to present you with my own conclusions, for what they are worth, concerning its real significance.

I will begin by frankly allowing that the historical element in religion is not there as pure history, in the sense in which alone Mr. Oakeshott, as we have seen, is prepared to use the word. Not because it is a record of *the* past, but because it is a record of the past of the religious society of whose tradition it forms a part, is it treasured by the society and held to be precious by its members. But, as I have already endeavoured to point out, without the interest felt by men in the past of the communities whereof they are members, the study and writing of what the modern scholar reckons as history in the proper sense would never have come into being; while it is normally with the arousing of such an interest in individuals that their dedication of themselves to historical study begins. It is true that, if a man is to become an historian in the proper sense, this original interest in the past of his own family or country, his own school or college or university, his own church or political party, while it may well continue to determine his choice of a special subject for investigation, must nevertheless cease to direct his attention to any portion of the relevant evidence to the exclusion of others, or to affect his judgment of its value as evidence. But the distinction of *history* from what we still call (using the word in an older and wider sense) "natural history" depends upon its concern with the *human* past;[1] while, again, the further distinction (which was present to the mind of Milton when he ruled out from history traditions of tribal warfare, which he held could not be distinguished from "battles of kites and crows, flocking and fighting in the air") rests, in its turn, upon a recognition of the continuity of a certain past with our own spiritual life—a recognition which Mr. Oakeshott must, I think, consider as irrelevant to the true function of history, and therefore, in a historian, illegitimate. The different "modes of experience," to use Mr. Oakeshott's terminology, are not after all, as

[1] Mr. Oakeshott (*Exp.*, p. 102) would deny that, except for convenience' sake, it is only so concerned.

he would have us believe, cut off each from each, in the old Greek phrase of Anaxagoras, "with a hatchet"; and it is, I am convinced, an error to suppose that, if one thinks that they are not so cut off, one is thereby precluded from understanding the distinct character of each and inevitably driven to confuse them inextricably with one another.

Yet, as I have already intimated, I should unreservedly admit that religion is not concerned with the past as such. It is concerned with the past of the religious man or religious community as affecting the religious life of the man or community in the present. Mr. Oakeshott has observed[1] that "Christianity seems almost from the beginning to have provided a new incentive for studying the past, but it provided no incentive for studying the historical past" (that is, the past as such). "It is only in recent times that a new and specifically historical interest has arisen in connexion with Christianity. And how great a revolution this has involved is known to those who have studied it in detail." These words afford a useful text for what I have to say in conclusion about the significance of the historical element in religion, and particularly in that religion in which, as I have already had occasion to observe, the greatest emphasis is laid upon it.

[1] *Experience and its Modes*, p. 105.

It is true, as I have already mentioned in my second Lecture, that the rise in modern times of an interest in what may be called history in the proper sense—the history not of *our own* past, but of the past *as such*, even where it is our own that we select for study—has profoundly affected—has, indeed, revolutionized—that study of its own past which Christianity has almost from the first promoted. That Christianity has been distinguished among religions by this encouragement of the study of its own past is to be accounted for by two facts. Of these two facts, one has to do rather with the circumstances of its promulgation, the other with an essential characteristic of its message. To take the latter first, the affirmation that Jesus Christ had come in the flesh, that the Saviour from the power of sin and death, whom it proclaimed, was no beneficent element in nature (like the sun), no mythical hero (like Mithras), no purely ideal figure (like the wise man of the Stoics), but a real person who, at an assignable date, had "appeared in Judaea,"[1] and of whose life, and especially of his death and resurrection—since it was on the ground of these that he was regarded as a Saviour,—credible witnesses could be produced; this affirmation was a fundamental tenet of Christianity, in the strength of which, during the earlier centuries

[1] See Burkett, *The Religion of the Manichees*, pp. 38 ff.

of its existence, it fought and conquered its rivals for the spiritual allegiance of the Roman Empire. It is obvious that, this being so, the traditional account of these happenings came to possess an importance for Christians which the story of one who was only a teacher or an exemplar would not have had. To suppose, indeed, that Jesus could be what he has been and is to Christians apart from the teaching attributed to him, and from the "holy life" which the evangelists describe, would be a profound mistake. The position now held in the world by the religion named from the title which his first disciples gave him could not have been attained and maintained by the proclamation of any other Lord than one whose life and teaching were such as the life and teaching of Jesus are said to have been. That teaching and that kind of life are what they are, and would not lose their excellence though we did not know who taught the one or doubted whether anyone had ever lived the other. Indeed, were their excellence merely an inference from the doctrine held concerning the person whose teaching and life they were, the teaching and the life would not themselves be available as Christian evidences. Yet a Christian who should say, "It matters not who taught this—I thought it was Jesus, but I may be mistaken about that—it is the teaching itself that matters"; or,

"Perhaps Jesus did not live thus, but this is the kind of life that I see it is best to live"—such a Christian would not be keeping all that is essential in a Christianity which could have won the position now held by it among the world's religions. Although what is called "the divinity of Christ" is not, without risk of destroying the substance of Christianity, to be separated from the ethical quality of his life and teaching, it belongs no less to the essential character of this religion to recognize in the appearance of Jesus in this world wherein we live the presence therein, not of one more seeker after God, but of God manifest in the flesh in the person of his Son. The phrase "God in history," which Mr. Oakeshott dismisses as meaningless, is one which a Christian can scarcely treat so cavalierly, though he may be constrained to allow that it needs not a little examination and criticism before he can adopt it as, in the phrase of to-day, a slogan for his theology.

I have now called your attention to the fact connected with an essential feature of the Christian message which I said was to be borne in mind in attempting to explain why Christianity afforded to a degree unparalleled by other religions an incentive to the study of its own past. It remains to mention the other fact which I said should be placed alongside of this, and which has to do not so much with an essential feature of Christianity as with the circumstances of its original promulgation. This was the connexion of Christianity with the past of a people other than that among whom it eventually made its home.

Christianity arose among the Jews, but very soon came to find its principal field for expansion in a world of men and women for whom the Jewish traditions which had moulded the lives of its Founder and first preachers, and which were presupposed by its rules of conduct and modes of worship, were something alien and unfamiliar. Moreover, it inherited a sacred literature to which the first Christians, being Jews, not only attributed a very high degree of authority, but were accustomed to appeal as affording prophetic evidence of the interpretation put by themselves upon the events in which the Christian Church had its beginning. The narratives of the Old Testament were presented to Gentile converts to Christianity for the first time as a history of the past of the new community—a community wholly unconnected with any to which their forefathers had belonged—into which they had by their baptism obtained admission, and as invested with the prestige of the sanctity already attributed to them by their Jewish teachers. So presented, it was natural that they should be received by those converts with a veneration, and studied with an attention all the greater that they were commonly regarded as containing the only authoritative records of a past more ancient than any commemorated in the literature of Greece and Rome—a past, moreover, which was professedly the past, not merely of a particular nation, but of the whole human race.

It is scarcely, indeed, too much to say that the whole conception of human history as a single and unique process of events in time, in which every past happening has its position and date, and no part of which is wholly unrelated to any other, is a product of Christianity, with its doctrine of the unity of the race which was created by God, fell in Adam, was redeemed by Christ, and the drama of whose life on earth is to be closed by the Redeemer's return to judgment. But just for this very reason the progress of historical knowledge has led to a crisis affecting Christianity far more seriously than it would have affected a religion concerned only with timeless truths illustrated by undated stories, and not appealing, as Christianity appeals, to the authority of Scriptures understood to describe the actual past and to foretell the actual future of the whole race of mankind and of the world which is its dwelling place.

The credit of these Scriptures as an inspired source

of information respecting the past and future of that world and its inhabitants was severely shaken by the great advances in geological and biological science which were made during the nineteenth century. Yet it is probable that, so far as natural science alone is concerned, a working compromise between the acceptance of the new knowledge and the traditional view of their authority might have been established, similar to the accommodation effected by an earlier generation of Christians, which had found it possible, by taking the Bible language as adapted to our everyday apprehensions, just as is that used in common life when we speak of the sun rising or setting, to adopt without reserve the principles of the Copernican astronomy. But the parallel progress of historical criticism was bound to disturb far more profoundly the attitude of educated Christians toward the sacred writings. The application to these of principles accepted everywhere else as applicable to the study of ancient literature has brought about (as I have already observed in my second Lecture) a revolution, than which Christianity has probably known none more complete—though others have been more spectacular, because accompanied by greater changes in ecclesiastical organization and in the external forms of worship and piety—since the Church was compelled to abandon the expectation

F

of her Master's return in the lifetime of the generation which had seen him in the flesh. On this occasion I am, of course, only concerned with the effects of this revolution on our attitude towards the biblical narratives as sources of *history*; not with its effects on our estimate of the authority to be attributed to the moral or metaphysical teaching contained in the Scriptures, though these last-mentioned effects have doubtless been no less important than those which are now engaging our attention. I myself, at any rate, have no hesitation in saying that the studies and discoveries of the last hundred years have given us a greater familiarity with the ways in which men felt and thought and wrote in earlier times, a closer acquaintance with the cultures and civilizations which were the background of the events mentioned in the Old and New Testaments; a much extended knowledge of institutions, customs, stories, beliefs analogous to those contained in the Bible; and a better-informed insight into the psychological habits of human beings, such that we can no longer regard as unique, mysterious, or insusceptible of any but a supernatural explanation, many things which to our forefathers it seemed quite reasonable to look upon in that light. Nor in particular can we avoid realizing that the aim of the professedly historical writers whose work is included in the sacred volume was in no case the writing of what would now be called objective history. The scholar of to-day will no doubt estimate by canons generally recognized in the learned world the trustworthiness of one such author as greater or less than that of another; but nowhere will he look for the dispassionate curiosity about the past, as such, which animates the modern historian. He will recognize that the ideal of the Scriptural writers was quite different: it was rather the joy of showing to the generation to come the praises of the Lord and his strength and his wonderful works that he hath done,[1] or of confirming one's fellow disciples in the faith that Jesus is the Son of God, and that believing they might have life in his name.[2]

The value of the historical element in religion is thus rather what may be called in a large sense of the word practical, rather than strictly historical. But this statement must not be misunderstood. Its "practical" value must not be taken to consist merely in the illustration of principles, or in the inculcation of lessons of conduct. Such a value might attach to a tale or parable which made no pretence to historical truth, quite as well as to an account of something which really took place in the past. Were this the

[1] Psa. lxxviii. 4. [2] John xx. 31.

whole value belonging to the historical element in religion, religion would certainly do well to abandon all anxiety about "evidences" and to recognize that a fiction may serve as well as a fact to point a moral or symbolize an eternal truth. But this element has, I would submit, a further value, as the embodiment of what I will call, using a phrase which I must go on to explain, the *memory* of the religious society to whose past it relates.

Now it is obvious that *memory*, in the proper sense of the term, can exist only in the mind of an individual person and can be only of events which that person has himself experienced. A man may indeed suppose himself to remember something which, as a matter of fact, he did not experience; how this comes to happen it would be wandering too far from my present subject to consider here; but in such cases we should say that the person in question was mistaken; that he did *not* remember what he thought he remembered; just as, in general, we cannot speak of *knowing* anything which is not true; though one may *think* one knows something which, since it is false, one cannot really *know*.

No one then can *remember*, in the proper sense of that word, anything which, when it occurred, fell outside of his own individual experience. I will further take it to be a thing which would be granted on all hands that, in whatever sense we may ascribe what is sometimes called a "corporate personality" to a society or group of persons, there is no actual consciousness of this personality as one's own except in the several minds of individual members of such a society or group. Any consciousness of the personality of the group in the mind of an individual member thereof must thus, as it would seem, be a consciousness of something which, though it may be common to the experiencing individual with other members of his group, is actually now present in his individual experience. A common faith or a common purpose may be present in this way in the experience of many; but not in any experience which is not the experience of one of that many. Now a memory, though always itself a fact of present experience, is, I am prepared to affirm, essentially a present consciousness of something past as past, not (as some have held) only of some present image or effect of what is past. Thus, while what is remembered may well be some past experience which was shared with, and remembered as having been shared with, other members of a group, it can never be an experience which was not at one time an individual experience of the person remembering it.

Nevertheless, there is, I think, a sense in which to speak of the memory of a community is not a phrase without meaning. I believe that, when members of a group are conscious of *sharing* the passion or the resolve, the pride or the shame which is theirs, not as individuals but as members of that group, this experience is really what it is thus described as being the experience of a common life, a common interest, a common good or ideal. I am disposed to ascribe to that sense of the past of a community which so often inspires and shapes experiences of this kind an evidential value beyond that which could be assigned to the grounds which an individual inspired by this sense could allege in support of his conviction that this past was of a certain character. Such an individual cannot indeed say that *he remembers* what happened before he was born; but his participation in a life which owes its character, or in a sentiment which owes its intensity to a tradition about the past of the society whose life he shares, gives him a legitimate ground for the conviction that this past was at least so far what tradition affirms it to have been, as to have been able to inspire the sentiment and to form the character, the reality of which he knows, as it were, from the inside. This conviction is, doubtless, compatible with the acceptance of what an exacter searching of records and documents may show to have been apocryphal details; and in some cases these details may have become to such a degree consecrated by long-continued repetition, or by their association with institutions and customs endeared to many generations, that to call them into question may well be distressing to those for whom they are bound up with much that they most highly value in the life of the community. We may think, for example, of an instance to which I have already referred in my first Lecture: of the hold which the story of William Tell, a story which modern historians reject, has had over the imagination of the patriotic Swiss. Yet, if there was no William Tell, there was an Arnold of Winkelried; and, however the imagination may have dressed up the facts, to doubt that *some* heroic resistance offered by a mountain peasantry to external tyranny lies behind the formation of the Swiss nation, would be to make unintelligible its present consciousness of itself.

I do not indeed believe that it is possible to lay down in advance the limits within which the tradition of a community is, in any particular case, to be trusted; any more than one can do this in respect to the individual memory, between which and the tradition of a community I conceive an analogy to exist which is more than purely verbal. No one who reflects upon such matters can have lived to be old without discovering how often even what he has taken to be a genuine recollection may be discovered, when tested by a contemporary record, a letter or a journal, to be inaccurate, and that even in points on which he has been accustomed, in relating it, to lay stress. Yet he does not lay aside, on that account, that general confidence in his memory without which his whole mental life would fall into ruins. Nay, even if one bears in mind the possibility of such hallucinations of memory as George IV's belief that he fought at Waterloo (and this seems, from a story told, I think, by Creevey, not to have been that monarch's only delusion of the kind), one is no more justified in wholesale distrust of what a man tells us that he remembers than one would be justified in wholesale distrust of his statements as what he is at the present moment feeling or perceiving. It would obviously be unreasonable not to recognize that the possibilities of error in a tradition are far more extensive and various than in an individual reminiscence. Yet I do not believe that it is in accordance with common sense to set no store—or even to set so little store as some eminent critics of Christian tradition have been prepared to set—on the constant tradition of a community as to the past of its continuous life. The historical element in religion is a tradition of this kind. It can never substantiate a claim to be history in the modern historian's sense; it is confessedly the product of a community's tradition and (I would even venture to add) of its *sense* of its own past; but, for that very reason, it is an integral part of its consciousness of being a community with a life of its own in which its members share. While such a tradition is certainly not a sufficient guarantee of the actual past occurrence of even conspicuous details, it is yet a witness to the historicity of the general situation presupposed in the present consciousness of the community; and it is perhaps unnecessary to add that if there be a real difficulty in explaining otherwise the existence and character of the community, where these are attested by unquestioned evidence, this fact affords an important corroboration of the tradition in question.

My main subject in these Lectures has been the historical element in religion in general, and it is no part of my present business to estimate the value of the narratives which constitute the historical element in Christianity. I would, however, ask you to recall what was said in the second Lecture of this course in explanation of the peculiar importance attached by this religion to its historical element. We saw that this is closely connected with its claim not to disclose abstract truths, ethical or metaphysical, nor even to call attention to particular impressive statements or striking illustrations of such truths, but to point to a single and unique process of divine self-communication. This single and unique process of divine self-communication admits indeed no genuine *alternatives* to itself, but is nevertheless capable of bringing in the end into organic relation with itself, and so including within its own system, other no less real but less central revelations of God, which may at first have appeared to be altogether separate and even discordant from it. As an increasing number of scholars, even in those schools of Christian thought which are reckoned among the more conservative, are now coming to admit, much that formerly passed for historical among Christian believers will not bear testing by the canons of modern historical criticism; nay, may in some instances turn out on closer inspection to be myth rather than history. Yet I believe that there is no reason why Christians should abandon what cannot be abandoned without the loss of something essential to Christianity, namely, its conviction that a continuous life links the Church of to-day with the little company of those who acknowledged in their crucified Master, now, as they were assured, risen from death to a new and immortal life, the exalted Son of God, whose spiritual presence was the inspiration of their life now, and at whose return in glory, expected at no great distance of time, they would be translated into the blessed conditions associated in Jewish tradition with the reign of the Messiah. The fashion of this hope, as well as much else in the faith of that early community, has undergone profound changes during the period of nearly two millenniums during which the Christian Church has carried on the life then initiated. But the consciousness of continuity with it has, amid all the corruptions and developments, the vast movements of thought and feeling, the far-reaching controversies and divisions which have bid fair to change the face of Christianity beyond all recognition, never departed from the society or group of societies whereof that community was the germ.

A contemporary school of philosophical theologians in Germany, of whom the best known in this country is Karl Heim, has urged, I think with justice, that theories of knowledge have been apt to make too little of the fundamental relation involved in the mutual intercourse in which men call each the other *Du*, *thou*. They have tended to treat men, as it were, from the outside, from the standpoint of the third person, for whom each is only *Er*, *he*. They have failed to recognize that in personal intercourse, in the act of mutual conversation, we have a revelation of a deeper or, if we will, a higher plane of spiritual existence. It will be obvious how this line of thought, applied to the philosophy of religion, will suggest that it is in communion with God—where we, as it were, hear him speaking to us and ourselves address him in prayer—rather than in the speculation for which he is merely an object of thought, that we come nearest to knowledge of the divine nature. I am myself much in sympathy with this way of thinking, which I mention here for the following reason. It might seem at first sight that, if religion is above all things an experience of communion with One who is at once the ultimate reality behind all our various other experiences, and also so intimate to us that even in our inmost being we are not divided from him—then religion is something which can very well dispense with what I have called an "historical element." But in fact it is the conception of religion which finds in it the profoundest of all experiences just because it does not leave outside the concrete individual who *has* all the experiences— the "finite centre of experience," as Bradley calls it, which in his philosophy remains an inexplicable and mysterious surd—it is this conception of religion which agrees with the recognition of an historical element in religion, in the sense in which I have been in these Lectures interpreting the phrase. This is the sense of a consciousness of personal continuity with an actual life reaching back into the past, and shared with other members of a community, analogous to the individual's memory of his own past, which indeed itself may be described as an "historical element" in his individual experience. Emphasis on the historical element in religion and emphasis on personal communion with God go naturally together. They are both at their maximum in Christianity, because it is of the essence of Christianity to insist upon the reality and significance of human personality as guaranteed by the personal relation of the individual human soul to God in its religious experience. This personal relation itself is not to be regarded as a mere assumption for use in practical life, but rather as the point in our experience at which the nature of ultimate reality is most intimately revealed. We must never deny to the philosophical activity of the mind its proper function of elucidating and unifying all our experience. It is no part of my contention that any part of that experience should be considered sacrosanct and exempt from the criticism of philosophy. But I am convinced that the function of philosophy is misconceived where it is held that it can dissolve the reality of that spiritual life of personal intercourse from which indeed, because in it it lives and moves and has its own being, it takes that highly significant name which Plato gave to it— the name of Dialectic.

The historical element in religion is then, I submit, closely bound up with the nature of religion as the form of experience in which we divine the coincidence of that which would satisfy the demand of our reason for an object free from all contradiction and unintelligibility with that concrete reality of which we inevitably find our standard in our consciousness of self. I say that we divine it, not that we apprehend it: for our communion with God in this life is not the beatific vision; yet only from accepting the former as a genuine experience can there spring up in our souls a reasonable faith in the reality of the latter.

V

In the foregoing Lectures I have endeavoured to state what seems to me to be the nature of the Historical Element in Religion, apart from any consideration of the bearing upon any controversial issue of the conclusions to which I have been led. I have found, however, that some who were interested by my manner of treating the subject were desirous to know how I should be disposed to apply my interpretation of the religious interest in history to some of those questions, which have been so often and so warmly debated among Christians in recent times, about the compatibility of the practice or profession of Christianity with doubt or denial of the historicity of certain alleged events connected with the origin of that religion. It is in view of such not unnatural curiosity that I add this supplementary chapter; but I wish to make it as plain as I can that I should not be inclined to abandon the position taken up in the Lectures—a position reached in independence of any inferences which might be drawn from it with regard to the particular beliefs hereafter to be discussed—because my opinions concerning these particular beliefs were found to be untenable. It is, moreover, very important, when dealing with such matters as those with which the following pages will be concerned, to keep carefully apart questions which are in fact wholly distinct, yet are apt to be mixed up together, because they are relevant to the same practical problems. For example, the question of the legitimacy of requiring from all who profess a certain religious faith, or at least from those who undertake to teach it, a declaration of belief in certain alleged historical facts, may be a very important question; but it is quite distinct from the question which I have been trying to answer, as to the nature of the interest of Religion in History, although no doubt the answer given to this last question may in the long run affect that which is given to the former. No less distinct and more remote from our present enquiry is that concerning the morality of using formulas which are or may be understood to imply a belief other than that actually held by the user. Urgent as this last question may become for this or that person, it is entirely irrelevant to the problem which is the topic of the earlier part of this book; and I shall say nothing about it in this supplementary chapter. I shall confine myself entirely to the discussion of the bearing of the view already put forward of the nature of the Historical Element in Religion upon our estimate of the religious value of belief in certain alleged events connected with the origin of Christianity, the historicity of which has, as a matter of fact, been called in question, although belief in them has been intimately associated with some of the most deeply rooted traditions of this religion, which (as we have seen) is distinguished among the world's great religions by the value set by its adherents upon the credibility of its sacred books. Such alleged historical events are the virgin birth and resurrection of Jesus, his institution of the Eucharist, and his commission, commonly called the delivery of the keys, to Peter.

In regard to the first two of these, an element enters into the discussion of their historicity which is absent from that of the other two—namely, their "miraculous" character. The additional difficulty caused thereby in accepting them as historical facts is, I think, unaffected by the considerations put forward in the preceding Lectures. Anyone who holds miracles to be *a priori* impossible or (with Hume) that no evidence could be sufficient to make credible the occurrence of one, must regard as mistaken any belief that these events actually took place. For anyone, on the other hand, who holds that miracles may be accepted on evidence sufficient to justify belief in a non-miraculous though very unusual event, the possibility that they did actually take place will remain open.

In respect of the first alleged event which I chose for examination, it will probably be widely acknowledged that the evidence for the virgin birth of Jesus is insufficient to compel assent, apart from any confirmation such as is, of course, afforded by its assertion in the Bible and in the Creed for those who, on other grounds, are prepared to accept Bible or Creed as possessing infallible authority. The fact that this particular story is of a kind, compelling evidence of which would in any case be peculiarly unlikely to be forthcoming, may be thought to make it reasonable to hestitate before dogmatically denying it; but it cannot make it reasonable to regard it as even probably true. What bearing, we have now to ask, will our previous discussion of the Historical Element in Religion have upon the question of belief in this tradition? It seems to me that it will have but little. Confessedly the tradition, while apparently well-established in the Church before the close of the New Testament canon, did not, according to the testimony of the New Testament itself, form a part of the original preaching of the Christian Gospel. Belief in it can thus hardly be held to be presupposed in the reception of that Gospel as a divine revelation.

Rather does the interest in the parentage of Jesus, to which were due the enquiries answered by the narrative of his virgin birth—and also (it must be added) the predisposition to find something exceptional in the circumstances of his appearance in the world which doubtless aided in winning credence for that narrative—presuppose the acceptance of Jesus by the Christian community as Lord and Saviour. Many conservative theologians would allow that, however congruous with his character as Lord and Saviour such a miraculous origin of his human nature may seem to them to be, his claims to that character would not be necessarily invalidated by any other parentage than that which tradition has ascribed to him. If this be so, the recognition that there is in the Christian religion an historical element which cannot be eliminated from it without fatal consequences to its claims does not involve the acknowledgment that the virgin birth of Jesus is an essential article of its creed. But, once more, I would earnestly deprecate the suggestion that the correctness of the view which I have taken of the general nature of the Historical Element in Religion, and especially in Christianity, is bound up with my own or any other particular opinion concerning the traditional account of the birth of Christ and its place in the system of Christian doctrine.

The same caution applies to the remarks which I shall now make on the next alleged historical event of which I propose to speak—the resurrection of Jesus. But here, if anywhere, we have to do with the historical element in the Christian religion, in the sense in which I have been using this phrase. For from the very first the Christian community has regarded and still regards itself as a fellowship established by One who "was dead and is alive for evermore,"[1] and its function in the world as that of a witness to the reality of that risen life. I have already pointed out[2] that the Godhead attributed by the Christian Church to its founder has inevitably invested the records of his earthly life with a significance beyond that which can belong to those of the life of any founder of a religion, however deeply venerated, for whom his followers have not made this supreme claim. It was not, it is true, until after centuries of controversy that the claim was formulated as it now appears in the Catholic liturgies and creeds; but an unique sonship to God was from the beginning attributed by Christians to Jesus; and it was, as St. Paul puts it, "by the resurrection from the dead" that he was "declared to be the Son of God with power."[3] A Christianity without the belief in the resurrection of Christ as an historical event would be another

---

[1] Rev. i. 18.   [2] Above, pp. 43 ff.   [3] Rom. i. 4.

Christianity than that which the world has hitherto known; and if a mistaken belief in his resurrection could have created it, the discovery of that mistake must inevitably deprive the Christian Church, wherever this discovery was itself believed and taken seriously, of the abiding inspiration of its religious life. Whatever else the "historical element" in Christianity may comprise, it must certainly be held to comprise the resurrection of Christ; or, to put the same truth another way, if any alleged historical events can be of religious interest to the Christian, it is this. But we have now to ask, what do we mean here by "the resurrection of Christ"?

In dealing with this question, I do not propose to examine the records of this alleged event with a view to discovering what precisely the evidence that they afford will justify us in asserting to have occurred during the period immediately following the death of Jesus upon the cross. I am concerned here with History, in accordance with the results of the discussion in the foregoing Lectures, only so far as it is an element in Religion. To say this is not (as has been suggested) to affirm that there is more than one kind of History, but only that there is more than one kind of interest in History. One is not suggesting that there are two kinds of Astronomy if one recognizes that a historian who is interested in the fixing or confirmation of a date by the astronomer's computation of the return of a comet may be content with the knowledge that a comet was observed at such a place and time, and may regard as irrelevant to his purpose problems about the comet thus observed which may be highly interesting to the astronomer on whom he is relying for his information. We may take another illustration of a different kind. A very accurate and scholarly history of an ancient mansion might be written, the trustworthiness of which as a history of that mansion would be practically quite unaffected by the author's views of the character of some person, say Charles I, a visit paid by whom to the house in question might have been a very important episode in its history. Yet it might be evident from the book itself that these views were so one-sided that they must disqualify the writer from being accepted as competent to write a judicious account of the conflict of Charles I with the Parliament. This last illustration is, indeed, much to my present purpose. For the sacred historians whose writings are included in the Bible were very far from aiming at the provision of a disinterested history of past events; they would probably not have understood the modern historian's ideal of an impartial estimate of all available evidence.

What we find in the accounts of the resurrection of Jesus is obviously, from the modern historian's point of view, full of difficulties, which there is no probability that any further investigation at this distance of time could entirely remove. Christian scholars will, notwithstanding, continually renew their efforts to examine these accounts, and will do their utmost to satisfy their historical curiosity respecting events of such momentous import. Christianity, moreover, as a religion which holds One God to be the author of all good gifts, is interested in such efforts as in every form of the sincere pursuit of truth. But the strictly religious interest in these events does not demand that the historian's curiosity should be fully satisfied before faith is accorded to them. For there enters as an essential factor into this faith the Christian's present consciousness of participation in a life continuous with that life the manifestation whereof in the appearances of Jesus after his death is the only adequate account of the origin of the community through which it is in every generation mediated to the individuals who share it. This consciousness cannot, of course, guarantee the historical accuracy of the details of the records of that manifestation; on the other hand, it would be misleading to dismiss its evidence as being evidence not of a resurrection but only of a (possibly mistaken) belief in a resurrection. There is no evidence which rests at any point on the credibility of witnesses which is not exposed to the abstract possibility that these witnesses were mistaken in what they believed themselves to have experienced. In the case of Christ's resurrection it is admitted, and even insisted upon, in the New Testament records themselves, that the risen Christ was manifested not to all the people, but to chosen witnesses.[1] It is still true, and no wise apologist for Christianity will desire to deny it, that there is no sufficient evidence that Christ is risen which could convince a doubter altogether apart from a perception of the quality of that life the secret whereof is found by those who partake of it in "the power of his resurrection."[2] But those who do perceive this quality are, I believe, justified in professing their confident persuasion that only a genuine experience of intercourse with a living person victorious over death can lie behind the original creation of the Christian Church, its continuance and frequent revivals during the succeeding centuries, and the renewed sense to-day in many quarters—and those in no wise out of touch with what is most vital and free from prejudice in contemporary life and thought—that in the Christ, whom the Church proclaims as the supreme revelation

[1] Acts x. 41. [2] Philipp. iii. 10.

to men of a God who is Spirit, lies now, as so often in the past, the only hope of a world seeking salvation from fear and despondency in face of a universe whose physical immensity threatens to reduce to insignificance the human spirit, which yet can never abandon its consciousness of superiority to all that is not spirit.

I have chosen the words "a living person victorious over death" to express my meaning, because I am convinced that neither communication, imagined or real, with the ghosts of departed friends and teachers, such as engages the attention of the Society of Psychical Research, nor the recognition, however devout or even passionate, of the undying value of the treasures of truth, beauty, and goodness bequeathed to mankind in the wisdom, the art, and the recorded conduct of the great spirits who have sojourned among us and then passed from our world never to return, is really comparable with the experience which finds expression in the stories of the first Easter. Confused and inconsistent as these no doubt are, the experience which they suggest is again and again repeated in Christian souls who worship him who "liveth and was dead and is alive for evermore." Precisely what past facts are necessary to account for this experience is a question which admits of differences of opinion. Whether the disappearance of the body of Jesus from the tomb in which it was laid, or the appearance of a palpable body, such as some of the New Testament narratives describe, are required as antecedents, and whether, if not, the evidence at our disposal is otherwise sufficient to justify us in believing them to have occurred, I do not wish now to discuss. What I would confine myself to asserting, on the strength of the principles maintained in the earlier part of this book, is that the specifically Christian religious experience is one of sharing in a life, the whole significance of which lies in its origin from the actual historical manifestation of One who had passed through death into a higher life and can impart to those who are in communion with him the principle of this life, so as to enable them to determine in accordance therewith their reactions to their earthly circumstances. The resurrection of Christ, so understood, and neither identified with mere survival of bodily death nor taken as a symbol for the permanence of intellectual, moral, or aesthetic values, is thus a reasonable object of faith for those who share this specifically Christian religious experience. The continuity within the community which claims to have originated in the experience of intercourse with the risen Christ, and of whose beginning no other satisfactory account can be given, of a distinguishable type of religious experience, renewed

from age to age in a great variety of contexts, cultural
and psychological, appears to me to afford evidence
of a kind which amply warrants those who share this
experience themselves or whose contacts with others
who share it has convinced them of its genuineness
and peculiar quality, in affirming their belief in the
reality of those historical antecedents without which
its existence would be inexplicable.

The third alleged historical event which I propose
to discuss was the institution by Jesus of the Eucharist
or Lord's Supper. This event is, of course, very closely
connected with the last which I have been considering.
Indeed, the practically undoubted fact that this cere-
monial meal has from the earliest days of Christianity
been the centre of Christian worship is one of the most
striking indications of the continuity of the Christian
Church with the original band of disciples who accompanied Jesus in his journeys about Palestine; and the
observance of it has been commonly regarded as the
principal means of communion with that same Jesus
as the crucified and risen Lord whom the disciples are
said to have recognized "in the breaking of the bread."[1]
But the records contained in the New Testament of
the institution of this meal as a memorial of himself
at his last supper with his disciples, when they are

[1] Luke xxiv. 35.

studied according to the usual principles of critical scholarship, leave it doubtful how far the declaration of an intention to establish a permanent rite, which is found in some of the narratives, belonged to the original tradition or was reflected back from the belief of days when it had become such. In view of the immense significance which has been by a majority of Christians attached to the Eucharist as the principal vehicle of the perpetual presence of their divine Lord in the society which he founded, the question has naturally been regarded by some as highly important how far the tradition that it was instituted by that Lord as a means of communion between his disciples and himself can be considered as authentic. It is to be noted that this question is not complicated by any difficulty arising from the miraculous character of the event concerned. The doubt is entirely created by the application of the methods of modern critical scholarship to the New Testament writings and to the ancient liturgies of the Church. For these last do not always emphasize the association of the Eucharist with the death of Christ as much as one would have expected had their compilers believed it to have been originally instituted as a memorial of it. Here I should be disposed to say that, on the principles defended in the foregoing Lectures, these very variations in the tradition upon which criticism has fastened do but strengthen the claim of the Eucharist to have been from the very first the outward expression in worship of the common life of the Christian brotherhood, intimately associated, in the minds of the original disciples, with memories of their Master's characteristic ordering of their common meals with him during his earthly life.

It seems to me personally more probable than not that at the Last Supper words were uttered by Jesus which justified the subsequent connexion with these memories of common meals with their Master of a further association with his imminent death conceived as a sacrifice inaugurating the New Covenant. But I should consider the purely religious interest in the historical truth of the traditional account of the institution to be satisfied by the continuity of the custom with the solemn assemblies of those who had been disciples of Jesus and now believed him to be risen from the dead and as their glorified Lord to be spiritually present among them. As the number of professed Christians increased, as there came to be different groups of Christians who did not think and feel precisely alike, and as theological reflection on the experience of communion with God through the exalted Jesus developed, these changes would affect in this way or that their eucharistic worship and tend in the long run to deepen and enrich its significance. But this whole process, the details of which can in all probability never be fully recovered, presupposes throughout a real continuity of the life and worship which has centred about the Eucharist with the inter-course of Jesus and his disciples—a continuity which can be admitted even by scholars who, on critical grounds, hesitate to assert the "dominical institution of the sacrament" in the strict and traditional sense of that expression.

The narrative of the delivery of the keys of the kingdom of heaven by Jesus to Peter is related by one evangelist only, and cannot on critical principles be regarded as among the best-attested incidents in the life of the Founder of Christianity. Great importance has come to be attached by one section of the Christian Church to this story, and far-reaching claims for Peter's supposed successors based upon it. It is obvious that the principles laid down in the foregoing Lectures afford no assistance in ascertaining the nature of the leadership which seems to have been enjoyed by Peter in the company of the first disciples of Jesus, the provision (if any) made for its transmission to his successors, or the persons (if any) in whom the succession to Peter was vested. I should, however, be inclined to affirm that the religious experience of many, though not perhaps of all Christians, involving, as it does, a consciousness of participation in a spiritual life proceeding from the risen Christ and mediated to them by the Christian society, the "body of Christ" whereof they are members, gives to the historical and juridical controversies concerned with the organization of that society—the solution of which is to be sought through the use of the methods generally applicable to such controversies—a genuine relevance to their religion. This fact imparts a religious significance to any evidence which may be produced in support of the assertion that certain institutions are or are not intimately associated with the maintenance of the Christian type of religious experience. As bearing, therefore, on this evidence, the properly historical question of their origin or continuity comes indirectly to possess a certain (and that a religious) importance to others than professed historians.

In this supplementary chapter I have considered four instances of alleged facts, connected with the origin of their religion, which have been generally believed by Christians. I have tried to show what bearing, if any, the views taken in my Lectures of the Historical Element in Religion would have upon the attitude to be adopted towards them by persons professing Christianity. No apology is, I think, needed for confining my attention to instances of supposed facts associated with the origin of this religion, since it is not only the religion most familiar to myself and to the majority of my readers, but also, as we saw, among the great religions of the world, admittedly that one which has attached most importance to belief in certain historical happenings.

My contention is that, when we ask what interest a Christian, as such, should have in believing such events as those discussed in this chapter to have actually occurred, we ought not to take up a certain attitude which has often been taken up in this connexion. We have no right to assume that a Christian can only be justified in so believing if he has, either antecedently to becoming a Christian or on resolving to continue one, made up his mind upon the balance of evidence for and against the occurrence of these events, as upon a problem proposed by a professor of history to his pupils; or, alternatively, if he is prepared to deny that the affirmation of historical facts, except as symbols of eternal truths, forms any part of his religion. I hold that it is only as asked by one who is in some real sense already a sharer in the life of the Christian society—even if only as having been brought up from childhood to conform to its customs—that the question about the necessity of belief in these events has any religious character at all. It is because, and only because, such belief may seem to be involved in living as Christians that there can be a religious interest in maintaining it. But, on the other hand, if the Christian life is one whose inspiration is largely drawn from the sense of belonging to a society with a certain past, it is not indifferent to him who is called upon to live it whether the past of this society was really what it has been believed to be. Now, when once the modern critical view of historical evidence has taken possession of the mind, one cannot with a good conscience withdraw from its scrutiny the alleged past of one's religious society. But, on the other hand, it may well be that what is essential to justify the present claims and the present attitude of the society is independent of such accuracy in the traditional records as would satisfy a modern critic in accepting them in all their particulars. The inclusion of such records in canonical scriptures or in credal formulas was accomplished by people whose conception of historical evidence was very different from that of an historical scholar of to-day, and whose intention was not to give a disinterested and objective account of the past for its own sake, but to affirm what they took to be the implications of a present religious

H

consciousness which they called upon others to share
with them. What is asked of sharers in that experience
(and of them only) is to affirm their belief in a past
without which the experience in question would not
be what it is. The possibility that the reality of this
alleged past might be actually disproved cannot indeed
be denied. Did this happen, our judgment of the
experience itself would unquestionably be affected.
We should either be compelled to confess ourselves
to have been the victims of an illusion in supposing
ourselves to have had the experience at all, or to have
been so far mistaken as to its origin that in future
we should react quite differently to it. In the first case
we should be in the position of a man who dreams
that he has the love of wife and children and awakens
to the reality of loneliness; in the second case, in the
position of the Lord of Burleigh's peasant bride, who
discovered that the true situation of the object of her
affections was so different from what she had supposed
that her whole behaviour must be changed. But it may
very well be that no such revolution is rendered
necessary by the frank recognition that the details of
a sacred narrative are in many respects suspect to an
historical critic, since there may yet be no ground for
doubting the truth of its main purport; and this may
be confirmed for those who share the experience of a
common religious life by the consideration that only

on the supposition of such a past is that experience intelligible.

It will be obvious to those who observe what William James called "the varieties of religious experience" that there is a great difference, as among religions, so among the adherents of a religion which embraces men of very diverse temperaments and trainings and degrees of culture; and that only for relatively few persons will doubt about the historical antecedents of their present experience have the importance which it certainly has for some. I would urge in conclusion that it is in the true interest of such a religion as Christianity, where, for reasons outlined above, this doubt is especially likely to arise, neither to crush it as sinful disloyalty to authority, nor to treat the problems presented by its traditions to the historian as though the practice of the religious life must be postponed till they are solved in abstraction from the experience which alone gives to them a religious significance. Neither obscurantism nor indifference is the attitude towards historical problems which is to be recommended to persons professing Christianity as that which is in genuine accordance with the spirit of their religion; but rather the faith which shrinks neither from the light of knowledge nor from the claims of love, because it is secure in the freedom which is the inheritance of the children of God.

INDEX

OVERLEAF

particulars of publications
of similar interest
issued by

GEORGE ALLEN & UNWIN LTD
LONDON: 40 MUSEUM STREET, W.C.1
LEIPZIG: (F. VOLCKMAR) HOSPITALSTR. 10
CAPE TOWN: 73 ST. GEORGE'S STREET
TORONTO: 91 WELLINGTON STREET, WEST
BOMBAY: 15 GRAHAM ROAD, BALLARD ESTATE
WELLINGTON, N.Z.: 8 KINGS CRESCENT, LOWER HUTT
SYDNEY, N.S.W.: AUSTRALIA HOUSE, WYNYARD SQUARE

Books by Clement C. J. Webb

Religion and Theism

Cr. 8vo.   4*s.* 6*d.*

"A masterly short book, and those who like a close argument . . .
will enjoy it very much."—*Times Literary Supplement*
"Mr. Webb vindicates the theistic claim and shows how in all
living religion the idea of a personal God is given and implicit."
Christian World

Group Theories of Religion and the Individual

La. Cr. 8vo.   6*s.*

"Contains much shrewd criticism. Especially interesting are the
pages on the connection between art and religion."—*Observer*

God and Personality

LIBRARY OF PHILOSOPHY

Demy 8vo.   *Third Impression*   12*s.* 6*d.*

"Mr. Webb, already in the front rank of philosophers, has greatly
enhanced his reputation and extended his influence by his admirable Gifford lectures. . . . All students owe him a profound
debt of gratitude."—*Daily News*
"Remarkable for its fresh and skilful handling of old questions, its
nimble dialectics, and its subtle insight."—*Holborn Review*

Divine Personality and Human Life

Being Part II of *God and Personality*

LIBRARY OF PHILOSOPHY

Demy 8vo.   *Second Impression*   12*s.* 6*d.*

"Mr. Webb writes with an easy mastery and a lucidity of style
for which we are grateful . . . everything he writes repays
thoughtful study."—*Methodist Times*

Religious Thought in France in the Nineteenth Century

by CANON W. J. SPARROW SIMPSON

Cr. 8vo.   5s.

"Dr. Sparrow Simpson writes from a well-informed mind . . . his judgments on men and movements are distinguished by sanity and a balanced spirit of scholarship."—*Church Times*

"An immense amount of information in a small space . . . in a style fresh and vigorous and with little display of bias . . . much that is as valuable as it is interesting has been included."—*Birmingham Post*

"It is beautifully written and is to be highly commended."—*Christian World*

The History of the Anglo-Catholic Revival from 1845

by CANON W. J. SPARROW SIMPSON

La. Cr. 8vo.   8s. 6d.

"A serious work of history dealing very fully with the doctrinal and legal aspects of controversies raised by the revival. It will take its permanent place in the literature of the movement."—*Manchester Guardian*

The Unitarian Movement in the Religious Life of England

by H. McLACHLAN, D.D.

Demy 8vo.   10s. 6d.

"An able exposition of the part played by Unitarianism in the religious, educational, and literary life of England during the eighteenth and nineteenth centuries."—*Birmingham Post*

"A mere glance at these pages is sufficient to show what immense and careful research lies behind them . . . lucid and orderly narrative."—*Manchester Guardian*

"In this book we have a valuable piece of cultural history, which needed to be written, and which has been done in most interesting fashion."—*Aberdeen Press and Journal*

The Modern Approach to the Old Testament

Cr. 8vo.   *by* JEWETT C. TOWNSEND   5s.

The Old Testament is full of problems which make its interpretation difficult even for scholars. In this book the author outlines and explains what these problems are, and how they can be considered.

Authentic history is distinguished from traditions, and the various books are so analysed as to present their definite contributions to religious truth. The manner in which the Bible grew and the processes of its compilation are so discussed as to bring out literary values and indicate its comparative historical and religious worth. The book is well indexed, and also contains carefully compiled and most valuable tables of dates.

Clergymen, all teachers of religious knowledge, and students who are studying the Bible will find this book invaluable.

The Heart of the Bible

by J. B. THOMSON DAVIES

Demy 8vo.   *In three volumes, with maps*   5s. each

"A most valuable book which, if it is given the chance, will really do what it sets out to do—reveal the heart of the Bible."—*Sunday Times*

"Excellent volumes."—*Christian World*

Old Treasure

A BIBLE ANTHOLOGY

Cr. 8vo.   *by* THE EARL OF LYTTON   3s. 6d.

"The editor has done a great work in a great way, and we cordially recommend this book to every thoughtful man and woman."—*Aberdeen Press and Journal*

"An inspiring treasury."—*Liverpool Post and Mercury*

Life Beyond Death in the Beliefs of Mankind

La. Cr. 8vo.   *by* J. T. ADDISON   10s. 6d.

"An excellently constructed and succinctly written piece of work . . . providing a survey of the principal beliefs about the afterlife as they have been held by all peoples of every religion, primitive and advanced."—*Inquirer*

Modern Tendencies in World Religions
by CHARLES SAMUEL BRADEN

La. Cr. 8vo.   10s.

"An impressive statement of the fact that it becomes increasingly hard to say from day to day what any of these great religions really are."—*Methodist Recorder*

The Social Triumph of the Ancient Church
by SHIRLEY JACKSON CASE

Cr. 8vo.   6s.

"The history of the Church's triumphant advent to security of the social side in ancient times . . . really interesting."—*Aberdeen Press and Journal*

The New Psychology and Religious Experience
by T. HYWEL HUGHES

Demy 8vo.   10s. 6d.

"An excellent volume, in which the teaching of the new psychology is treated with much patience and due respect in an admirable spirit of intellectual honesty."—*Scotsman*

"Luminous and profoundly interesting . . . the strength and appeal of the book, however, is in Dr. Hugh's own constructive thought."—*British Weekly*

A New Highway Towards Christian Reality
by T. WIGLEY, M.A.

La. Cr. 8vo.   8s. 6d.

"It is a thoughtful, broadminded contribution to our knowledge of God to-day, taking into account the assured results of the sciences . . . helpful and refreshing . . . a good, sound volume."
—*Friend*

All prices are net

LONDON: GEORGE ALLEN & UNWIN LTD